EDIT YOUR LIFE
—Design Your Destiny—
Say Goodbye to Depression

VEERACHAI JUNHUNKIT

Disclaimer:

Although all attempts have been made to verify the information provided in this publication, neither the author nor the publisher assumes any responsibility for errors, omissions, or contrary interpretations of the subject matter herein.

This book is for entertainment purposes only. The views expressed are those of the author alone and should not be taken as expert instruction or commands. The reader is responsible for his or her own actions.

Adherence to all applicable laws and regulations, including international, federal, state, and local laws governing professional licensing, business practices, advertising, and all other aspects of doing business in the U.S., Canada, or any other jurisdiction is the sole responsibility of the purchaser or reader.

Neither the author nor the publisher assumes any responsibility or liability whatsoever on the behalf of the purchaser or reader of these materials. Any perceived slight of any individual or organization is purely coincidental.

Table of Contents

DEDICATION

This book is dedicated to my wife who passed away in a fatal car accident in 1986.

Where my endless pain started and the beginning of trying to do Life Editing

Since our body can work on its own regardless of its state, whether we are awake or asleep, conscious or unconscious, our body never stops working. Life goes on non-stop through any condition to the end.

In this case, no one can refute the truth that there are some systems that control its works beside us! And it is this elusive system that let us live well, it also tries to devour our freedom all the time through different unwanted evil emotions that is so tough for us to strike back. These emotions express themselves as sufferings, pain, fear, sadness, grieve, greed, rage depression or even lovesick.

Our most desirable moments are when we manage to release all of these unwanted evil emotions that affect our happy life.

This book is intended to unveil this elusive system with the most profound guide on how to edit it.

—Veerachai

—— PART 1 ——
SUBCONSCIOUS

PROLOGUE

Before we can edit our life, the first question is 'Does our body and mind belong to us?'. If it does, 'Do we know how it works?'

Without the perusal of Anatomical or Physiological texts, can someone that is not medically inclined instantly describe how many parts or functions inside our body and how it works? If our body is a car, we can relate it as to a normal driver who only knows how to drive but don't know how it works or how to maintain it in a perfect condition. Though some Scientists or medic may have little knowledge on it, but there are still lots of mystery surrounding our body and mind including fate and destiny of every being, and a lot are still in ignorance. Some great physiologists said that they know everything after graduation, but know less after postgraduate, then lesser after Ph.D. and know nothing after being a Prof.

We may explain how our body works through Anatomy and Physiology, but how it behaves and the effect of behavior on one's life or destiny may still be in oblivion. Some try to explain it through Psychology but it's still intangible and ethereal. However, if we look in the way as to how behavior is processed by some sort of self-enhanced software inside our body, even at that it's still intangible and ethereal, however, we can vaguely see some logic and physic, like DNA coding, Amino, and Protein Programming. And if this is true, we may explain many phenomena in a more logical way.

In view of programming, basic software of everyone should be more or less the same on a basic factory setting but eventually gets enhanced or evolved according to our environment and lifestyle, like our computer that's more or less the same on ex-factory which have only BIOS (Basic In/Out System) which is the most profound idea of Biology, but later enhanced by Operating System like Windows on PC, IOS for Apple and Android on Mobile,and then with every other necessary software with specified requirements, regardless of Microsoft Office, Adobe or Macromedia.

According to life programming system, some persons develop to fight for everything, doing whatsoever they desire, some could develop in godliness with many morals and principles to follow, while some may develop to abscond from every problem.

To support each others behavior, the physical effect may follow as a chain.   One may have good muscle build and functionality if they are farmers, soldiers or labor workers, but one may have better brain functionality, if they are scientists, doctors or even office worker. Skilled work or behavior is being enhanced for more specific functionality on every single moment as its being used or expressed, as the guitar is played consistently it forms bumper on the finger with more sensitivity on sensing the stringed cord that makes us place our finger exactly on the spot without looking.

And this enhancement or evolution is where all kinds problem came from, this evolution develops wrongly when we lose control of its direction, as it is with Cancer, Stroke, Heart attack, Diabetes, Blood Pressure, Obesity, Parkinson, Alzheimer's including all Mental Illnesses like Depression or any evil emotions.

Now, if the above hypothesis of behavior generated by software is true, the question is "what program it is, who wrote it, how is it being written up, who did the enhancement, can we control its direction, or can we edit it"?

The most potential answer from what we know on today's science should be the 'Subconscious' since it also elusive and complex as a behavioral substance, even in self-developing in term of learning and response on survival instinct that mostly deal with autonomic nervous system through DNA coding, Amino and Protein programming, which is involuntary, and beyond our control,it tends to do everything on its own will, if we have no background on how it works to guide or edit it on a correct path.

Subconscious or Instinct is one of the three systems in our body which consists of Primal System, Subconscious, and Conscious. If Primal System is the operator, then Subconscious can be compared to a Supervisor or Manager whose functionality is direct control over operators.

Subconscious's duty is to conduct operations to work and fit for all situations or circumstances on the purpose of 'Survival' or 'Homeostasis' in term of physiology. The bump that forms on the guitar also started from pains on a fingertip and since this pain is under caution of survival, eventually the subconscious triggers dead cell from its disposal so as to keep it in, for being bumped instead. And this is one sample of enhancement.

Besides the subconscious, we still have 'Conscious' as Managing Director who is being affected regardless of happiness or pain. Conscious functionality is about learning, analysis, laying down policy and managing from the top. If this Managing Director which is the conscience doesn't do its job well, one will rely more on the subconscious to make a decision which relies mostly on emotion or instinct, instead of logical reasoning, and all disasters may come as the consequence and becomes its Fate.

Fate and Destiny could be in a dull state or foggy, no one exactly knows why someone gets HIV by chance, why someone gets involved in an accident by coincidence or why some do less and get big and some put all efforts, but luck never comes close.

If there is no logic behind through life's long journey, how can we be certain that we can evade all the dangers of fate?

By the way, there is some clue in there, that fate should be related to the subconscious since fate or destiny is the direct causes of our behavior and behavior is generated by the subconscious.

A Fighter will not easily be turned to a peacemaker, their fate is being orchestrated to fight and they may have a high risk of brain cancer, hypertension or heart attack. But for the weak who always are in fear will hardly be turned to fight, however, the rate of depression would be high with them.

In this book, we shall not talk much about 'Primal System' which can find out easily on any anatomy or physiology texts, but we shall focus only on the elusive Subconscious that's fascinating, ambiguous in the relationship with our Consciousness over the control of our body and mind on every single moment.

Cardinally Let me show you some samples of the mysterious operation done by this elusive subconscious which consisting of Ignorance and awareness, so we can have more profound knowledge of how it works and affects our lives.

Chapter 1

CAN MILLIPEDE ACTUALLY HURT PEOPLE?

One fresh morning in July, Kate was jogging as usual. Though, today was different! she was dead - shocked by just a small millipede slowly crawling on a lower pavement by the road. Her reaction to this incident was quite terrible. Her Heart rate reading on her Garmin device worn around the wrist jumped up to the max of Zone 6! No blood shade could be found on her face. Faint and a fall could have happened at that moment.

"Let's take a rest first", I said. This state of shock always happened to Kate all the way around from her age of 10 to now, which I kept on talking with her that the problem is not real. "How can a millipede hurt you with its very low speed. Also, millipede cannot jump or fly or bite you on any occasion. What are the real reasons for being scared to death like this every time you see a millipede". At every time she was asked such questions her feedback was always "I don't know".

Now let's come together and see the reason behind the scene on what Kate was oblivious of, Talking about this scene, back to her age of 10, our family has one deserted building left unoccupied for a while, till one day there was someone interested to rent it, Kate and I went to that house for clean - up. As the door opened, a frightening shocking scene presented itself before Kate's eyes. Myriad of millipedes swarmed all over the wall that displayed a terrifying crimson luster flickering scenario like shocking nightmare scene in Alien's famous film. On that moment Kate stiffened and was dead-shock, her consciousness being taken over by the subconscious which suddenly became in charge once "conscious" can no longer function in its work properly according to the body surviving system, even as we are asleep or unconscious, the body keeps on their non-stop profound work to maintain self-survival e.g. breathing, digesting, data processing etc.

In Kate's case, her consciousness seized as a result of the shock which triggered the subconscious to rise to its work, that made any incidents carried on from that point till her recovery unaccountable to her conscious. The only memory remained was long-term memory that being imprinted on her subconscious, which is the reason that Millipede equals Death! We can comfortably say the Millipede was the trigger point to flip up her deep shocking memory to live beyond her conscious transcendence. And this is the reason why she cannot explain why millipede means death for her.

Since this is the case, how can a physiologist or a scientist know how to diagnose and cure this effects on her reactions towards millipedes. By the way, it's not like we have no way to tamed or control these feelings. Memory is not only created on an instant but through life's critical moments by taking charge of the subconscious over consciousness for security purpose, but can also create through long-term repetitive effect . For example, if we once saw the very scary movie that's haunting to the heart, we might not be willing to keep in touch with it further. But if we take a few more rounds on the film, may be up to 20 rounds, you will find out that the scary scenes indistinctly takes its effect on us. Furthermore, since we have begun to develop memory on it already, then the terror will have no further effect on us, thus confidently knowing it's not real that it's just a film. Such as the case, if we put a bottle made of transparent glass with millipede inside, then placed on our hand from time to time, we will find it's shocking effect becomes of no effect through the hands of time, usually our experience comes from repetitive learnings and memory until it overflows the previous memory/frightening effects that were created from the subconscious.

This kind of solution can also be applied to other cases of phobia created from deep memory, beside Millipede e.g. Lizard, worm or arachnid phobia or even the one who suffers from aerophobia

Chapter 2

SUDDEN SICKNESS

One Friday night, Harry prepared to take his family to see his mum usually after a protracted period, so the kids were so excited to have this long weekend trip. While Mary was in the kitchen, climbed up halfway on the ladder to put washed dishes on the upper cupboard, kids rushed in, running around and mad everywhere rowdy and noisy. Harry entered the kitchen, screamed at them as to get them out. At that moment, Mary happened to have fallen sick. She became unhappy, her face was pale, so white as paper. Mary suddenly lost her composition.

A few minutes ago, she looked healthy and strong with no signs of illness, what suddenly happened to her? This is not the first likely incident. Harry has taken her to many Hospitals on the area nearby, but all doctors informed the same that Mary is healthy, no illness could be found even to the slightest of them. Nevertheless, by Harry final effort on Dianetics Treatment, through hundreds of repeated questions and answers on what had happened in the kitchen before she got sick, Mary started to get mad on the questioner and unconsciously shouted at him, anyways with some clues added up, Mary referred that the pain was just like her head hitting on the floor, and this clues triggered up Harry long time memory on accident that once happened in the kitchen when Mary had fallen from a ladder and was knocked down on the floor in the midst of kids, as they were playing around and Harry scolded at them . By these final words, we eventually knew that Mary's illness was flipped up by her deep memory that was created from the subconscious because in that state of unconsciousness she went through severe pain.

Technically, once the subconscious takes charge, they are more direct than the consciousness, memory created by them is signal-wise, not event-provoking. In this case, the subconscious noted down that "frequency of kid's noise with Harry's scolded-sound plus the visual of the kitchen scenario" equals to "severe pain". Once those 3 factors happened to be matched, it simulated severe pain as pre-warning of danger to our conscious to act as if we are extremely in a serious situation of life or death.

For a solution, since this happened by ignorance, the symptom will trend to reduce through this transcendence of the root cause, thus it will cease to exist sometimes after a series of repeated actual incidents.

Chapter 3

VOLUNTARY AND INVOLUNTARY

Alice is a benevolent person, many foundations recognized her as a good supporter. She always paid big fund for charity including a few monthly supports for orphans. However, her fairy appearance does not lasts long all the times, especially when she bought something overpriced, and happened to know afterward. She will get mad at the one who takes chance on her then turn to be a witch at that certain moment. Her rages sored high, blood pressure rushed up to Zone 6 with the risk of faint or instant shock. This problem of hers happens intermittently, and efforts made to analyze the reactions towards the incidents that usually affects her body or mind. always being picked up from time to time to analyses on what functions of her body or mind.

Alice can donate big fund for charity without giving a sigh, but why would this little-overpriced matter hurt her to this extent. The reasons also fall back to the mysterious phase of 'ignorance'.

In this case, after several interviews on peoples who also was subjected to this syndrome, we found that the problem is not the value of money itself, it's the problem of pride and prestige as against mockery. 'Giving' feeds her pride while 'Being Cheated' or undue advantage attacks her ego. Value of loss in term of money may be humongous but the loss of face or mockery is infuriating as high to the sky. Hence this crazy attitude of Alice came from a profound command of the subconscious on the rule of pride or to be seen as a giver, perhaps to gain respect and power that feeds our ego, while being a victim of derision or loss on self-protection is a big caution on our survival potential.

Through down to the root cause of her usual crazy response to this peculiar incidents, if Alice can take this cheating as one of her giving transaction or charity works, there should be no further grudge on her mind, then the subconscious may release its constriction and put her heart free from constraints.

Chapter 4

SENSE OF OWNERSHIP

Susan is a car lover, her car is being kept in a good appearance and good condition all the time, no dirt is allowed even to a slight. She always keeps her car clear and clean to the tit even the engine chamber. Nobody can touch her car without her being anxious with her eyes fixated on the car. One day she got an accident on her way back home, her car had a little dent on the left front door, she kept on looking at it for a few hours with severe pain on her mind and tried every effort to rub it away but to no avail.

On the next day she couldn't endure this pain further, so she decided to sell it out.

On the car transfer day, after she got the money on hand and planned to get a new car, a big tree branch accidentally drops on the car after the buyer drove off from her house. The incident frightened Susan a lot, but no sign of mental pain as it used to be, the only sign of sympathy left in her eyes instead. This is the question of ownership and how it affects the body with pain or mental illness.

Firstly, we should understand how ownership works, Once we possess some properties, our memory will register on survival data tool marked as protected for the sake of survival. In this case, Susan's car being registered on her memory as a precious survival tool, it gave her convenience on energy saving in terms of traveling and represented her wealth and honor which lead to respect and power that directly connects to her self-worth and existence hence this car must be protected with utmost care.

Once it is sold off, the car is being disposed from her survival-tool database and would no longer trigger any sense of protection on her self-worth, after repeated incidents with the car, since the car's image that she saw this time cannot match with any assets data on hand,then Susan may not have such mental rage or illness.

In term of this, we may conclude that it's is only what is being identified as a survival tool can trigger our fight for protection or feel heartache once it gets lost or damaged, while no much feeling on others since it triggers nothing except we find that there will be some sort of benefit to show off a feeling of sadness or if we put ourselves in their shoes, this is the matter of Ownership.

Queuing is also another good sample of Ownership. Today's traffic was extremely in chaos, Sharon was in a gloomy and boring state owing to the fact that she has been held for more than 2 hours in the traffic, just 3-4 meters move per flow. Her icy cold eyes now glanced at one car in the left corner of her car, that was about to rush out once there is a flow. After a few minutes as the cars ahead moved, Sharon immediately moved over the car to head on just only 3-4 meters off with a ferocious acceleration. What is the benefit of this action? Why take such reckless action for just a 3-4 meters advantage over the car?.

The reason is due to the matter of ownership. Queuing is also an asset, even its ethereal but also registered on survival tools database since it can save time and energy while traveling which may affect another's benefit of some deal or prevent late Arrival which could have consequences.

From this, we can see that it's indeed not the matter of time or distance, but just the matter of ownership

Repeated transcendence of these root causes from time to time may trigger our consciousness and see the real deal that went on through our subconscious operation.

Chapter 5

WHO CONTROL'S US

Jeff still remembered the last time he had a squabble with his wife, the family was in a troubling state for nearly a month. He vowed from that time that there would be of no such incident that caused chaos happened again whether he was right or wrong, he would never shout at his wife again. This intention was intentionally repeated in his mind from time to time until one day his wife asked him about their plans for the coming long weekend so he suggested a few interesting places, which all were rejected, he got frustrated, and shockingly raised his voice at her like the initial time , and then with the same old cold-state back in place for the longest day as usual. Jeff was so dazzled and repeatedly asked himself of the cause of his reactions toward his wife. He surely doesn't know who did that, it's was surely not him.

Looking at this case, Jeff, full of consciousness is extremely not willing to let this matter happened, but the operation of the subconscious kicks in, And this is the question of ignorance on how the subconscious can alter jeff's intention. The Problem is that the moment Jeff gets mad and loses consciousness, his subconscious kicks in and takes the drive on its own will according to its profound knowledge to carry on live since Jeff's repeated actions of less conflict is still too weak compared to the fighting root that was implanted on his mind far longer.

Our body and mind work on a non-stop basis, the operation never stop even on sleep, that's why we still survive whether we have or no have conscious.

Chapter 6

GIVE and LOSE

The very famous fortune teller told Ben that he would loss $100,000 in a few days. This statement annoyed him for a whole day. He was so anxious about this loss until his mental health weakened and got exhausted. On next morning, he made decisive decision to cut loose of this amount by donating it out for charity. After doing so, he rejoiced from the praise and glory that emanated from a charity announcement of his benevolence.

Finally, he really lost those $100,000 with gladness instead of grieving. Mental or spirit can be pain or happy depend on what spot of our physical brain and how it's functioning. The reason behind this also is so identical to 'VOLUNTARY AND INVOLUNTARY' of Alice in the previous chapter, but different only on timing. In this case, the incident has not yet happened, but brain simulated situation which may occur and made a decision on simulation based on the same logic as Alice case.

Chapter 7

ONE ONLY KNOW HOW THEY ARE BEING TREATED

Maggie usually parks her car in front of her house. And she is always raged in the sky whenever she comes from work and finds someone's car parking in her place. The problem persisted on like this for a few days until one day she couldn't endure this further and decided to wait to meet the car owner. On that day, the car owner finally came back, she then approached him and shouted at him for always infuriating her by parking in front of her house. she got an answer that stunned her for a few minutes, could not find an appropriate answer to the man's response, the man said that "This is a public area, could you park and I cannot?. And if it has come down to the point that I angered you by parking in front of your house, then how about you infuriating others next to your house including me, as your car has deterred us for more than a year.

Eventually, Maggie realizes what blinded her from this simple logical reasoning. Why she had never thought otherwise. Isn't it that people always sense more on what is being treated to them but less on what is being treated to others.

This case is also like the carcase of Susan, Maggie ignored the right of others since it's not triggered by any survival protection on her subconscious, but instead, registered space in front of her house as her belonging and treated it as one of her survival tools collection that needed protection, since she will need more energy if she must park in a distance or waste money on the renting a car space .

If people can transcend how we don't want to be treated, others also don't want too, the world perhaps can live in peace and no war to fight.

Chapter 8

TIME OUT

Due to a very terrible traffic yesterday, Jim took more than 4 hours in his car on the way back from the office to his home.Indeed, there shouldn't be any problems if it was not the case that Jim needed to pee starting from the early of a second hour, however, the situation was still on an early state, not so severe. With the hope that only 20 miles left which normally shouldn't take longer than 30 minutes. But unfortunately, it took more than 3 hours after. At this point, Jim still can manage to endure even after the sensation had advanced to a more serious state. Finally, Jim arrived home on a super emergency state after 4.30 hours in total. On arrival Jim jumped out from his car with the door key in his hand and moved swiftly to the door on an Olympic Speed that's faster than whatsoever in 'Fast and Furious,' then passed smoothly through the door, just to find out that the Toilet is being occupied. Jim shouted out loud with all his might to the one inside to hurry up. Since, it's time out! Why are the anxiety and the rush being released in front of the toilets door?

The question that arises is that why can he patiently wait for over 3 hours and a half but cannot endure for just a few seconds in front of the Toilet.

This is also the problem of repeated command to the subconscious on the target to release its bowels when he gets to the toilet, in this case, the trigger is the toilet. Once the target is being fixed, and target hit which means that we have already arrived the toilet, our conscious then will enter a relieve state, near - sleep mode, the subconscious will flip up and trigger our release command instantly. Even our consciousness may want to respond but most likely its helpless because it's always on the next queue anyway. The command normally respond base on first come first served , especially direct command from the subconscious, except severe command of life or death may come a bit faster like someone stab a sharp pin on our arm exactly on 'Time Out', priority will instantly switch to push damn noise on that guy first and may even forget the problem of pee.

Chapter 9

HURRY UP BY INSTINCT

On a holiday of a long weekend, our family had the chance to take a trip to the northern parts. "Hurry up, it's too late," mum said. I just asked her in return that what is there to hurry up for, our resorts booking is late afternoon, even if we arrive there before noon, we will not be able to check in. She seemed to understand and that paused her from urging for a while, then back to push again for just a few hours later. I had to remind her again of the fact. However, she keeps on pushing like this from time to time, until I had to sit and talk to make it clear what is the reason beyond her mind. The answer is 'SHE DON'T KNOW'. It's naturally that her time is always extremely valuable to her daily work until she won't be able to persist after the time has elapsed and of no value.

For this case, it's clearly the work of that vulnerable-elusive subconscious since mum worked hard all through her life, time was never even enough for her. This consistent lack of time is being repeated and repeated to her subconscious from time to time until it was registered into her survival tools database. Hence, wasted time means loss of security, the subconscious must swiftly take charge in once mum distraught to manage time more valuable no matter what.

The Subconscious profound base is to work on the program while our consciousness works on reason. It is best if we can look at how our subconscious works and be more cautious on the result.

Chapter 10

MENTAL COLLAPSE

Sunny is a drunk, he used to be in the hospital many times due to 'liver cirrhosis'. Every time he stays there, between two to three days he could get back to work. This time also the same, he was admitted since last Saturday, many friends took a visit and chit chat with him on general matter. His overall look was not bad, we all thought that his sickness was caused by drinking too much as usual. However, he passed away on that night with reasons UNKNOWN.

According to the nurse, he was shocked after seeing the doctor's chart on top of his bed which showed his symptom was subjected to Cancer.

While he believed that his symptom was not big, his mental mind ignored all existing pains by giving credit to the familiar 'liver cirrhosis' which has no much threat on his life. However, hence the fact unveiled itself as Cancer, which his subconscious knew exactly that there was no cure, all pains flipped up instantly from normal to severe, with all vital signs being boosted up to the sky in an instant by the frightening of subconscious sudden command for an emergency state, that made the primal system decided to pack his life force and leave according to the rule of death which is the last survival tool of life on searching new body once vital signs overboard its limit and the body can no longer persist on.

This situation can apply to all sudden death from Shock!

Chapter 11

PHANTOM LIMB

One patient came to a hospital with severe pain on the left leg and the doctor had to cut it off while he was still in an unconscious state. After treatment, he recuperated after a few days, his wound recovered and closed up to normal, but he still did not know that he has already lost his leg.As the patient woke up with full consciousness, he kept on complaining of his pain on the missing leg, and doctor showed him that indeed, he had no leg already. He stiffened for a while and start crying again. He didn't know why, but he extremely feels pain on that spot as if it still exists.

The case of this patient clearly shows his consciousness is exactly aware that he had no leg further but his subconscious had not yet accepted the reality and registered with this new status and continued to send pain signal to the brain,but as it could not communicate with that limb, to drive the brain and body for whatsoever remedy since in some case those people whose limbs were cut off can still be fixed back by a doctor. The patient may keep on crying like this for a while until really no hope, maybe 4-5 months, then stop and accept the new status of no leg.

This kind of mental denial can not only be found in physical cases, even in mental cases of love can still be found. Once one loss their love, mental illness will persist to have their love back to life up to 4-5 months before it faded away. Anyway, we can be assured that it will cease to exist someday, every case always comes to the realization of its reality, since memory cell dies every day which we shall go in detail on the next chapter.

Chapter 12

LIFETIME STINGINESS

Grandma was very rich, at over 80 years of age, she kept on saving even as little as a cent as usual. If she wants something, her kids had to buy for her with their own money (she couldn't and will not buy it herself) and got her reprimanded on prodigal in return. Whenever they asked her "why she had to be like this since she has money more than enough for the rest of her life? ", she said that one must save to be rich but then she was asked why after being rich should there be a reason for such kind of saving? she couldn't give any answers but rebukes strongly instead.

A case like this makes us have A CLEAR picture of how the subconscious work. It represented all auto functions like 'Familiarity', 'Skill', 'Behavior', 'Habit', 'Temperament', 'Trait' or 'Instinct'.

If we keep up some repeated actions over a long period of time, the subconscious will note it down on their basic task which is preserved as an autopilot for us but is different from a case when the autopilot is being shifted by us intentionally. The subconscious triggers up and takes charge once it feels appropriate on its own will, like this case of stinginess. After long repeated attitude of Kathy on savings during her formative period especially on struggling from survival to a millionaire, her subconscious noted it down as the way to survival. Any actions against this, means loss or harm to her present status, her overbearing survival tool or autopilot under the control of her subconscious would flip up overboard and reject or fight back on its own, which lead to a reprimand as what had happened, even when it's not compatible to the real situation, since the subconscious regard only its own survival rule unlike the consciousness that has the ability to learn, to gain knowledge from environment and to simulate the situation which may happen through the incoming and existing data on our memory.

What is done by the subconscious under auto function, we may call it personality or temperament or even call it an instinct. But to what degree, it depends on how long our memory is being imprinted repeatedly on the subconscious.

Since autopilot act on its own internal long-term repeated memory which may not compatible with the real situation, however, nature still give us this function.

Beside the dark side of its stubbornness or overbearing responses, this function of autopilot is extremely necessary. We may not be aware of what this function assists or handle things for us. Let's see some sample of driving a car, many times we drive while we are on the call, the one who drives for us is not us, but the subconscious. Indeed, we really drive a car by ourselves only on training period that needed full concentration on collecting driving data, learning and experiencing many case studies in many situations, and repeat like that until subconscious noted it down then that becomes an involuntary skill of us. Very few people know about this, they still thought that they drive on their own. That's why once a situation happened out of frame, the subconscious has no solution for it while our consciousness focuses with the call on the phone, accident then occurs unavoidably.

If we think of what else autopilot do for us, we may think of it as tasks based on skills learned done involuntarily and that is what is being done by the subconscious which is hard for us to intervene if there is nothing beyond pattern. However, if one wants to fight back our free will on some tasks that being shifted over to the subconscious, one must put effort on a long-term plus repeated responses too, to build up another auto pathway which weight more in term of memory agglomeration.

Chapter 13

EXCITEMENT

Today John had to give a speech in front of more than a hundred audience, he was so excited, his body trembled and was cold. He had to go to the toilet many times since his arrival at the hall. He really didn't know why he was always shivering every time he is about to give a speech. He doesn't want to be like this, but this body of his was always beyond his control in such events.

Excitement is indeed a normal phenomenon which is able to happen to many people on an early stage of doing something that they care most about, the subconscious will place excessive concern on it and react on each similar situation with the same profound response. If one always choose to fight all problems, their subconscious will boost up energy all over body in blood boiled fashion which created heat, and perspiration on every pore as the consequent to ventilate extra heat from hardworking muscles or from overstimulated nerves in order to fight effectively, but if one always choose to flight, the subconscious will preserve all energy including increasing the body's temperature set-point from standard of 37 to maybe 38 up high that make normal body temperature of 37 or 37.5 become little low in order to simulate cold situation, hence trigger negative feedback on cold handling, starting from the brain signals the dermal blood vessels to constrict and causes the sweat glands to remain inactive for the body heat conservation which makes us pale, also the nervous system signals muscles to contract involuntarily to generate body heat that makes us tremble, and once no perspiration, the only choice to remove off water liquid from body is left over to the urinary tract.

For John's problem, in his first speech, he was cold and trembling, thus wanting to pee as normal to ease out the tension. If he can endure to the last minute and run smoothly with his topic, that will be fine, next time he will be less excited and be better since the experience is being developed through repeated conscious effort. Unfortunately, on this first time, he couldn't endure to the end, even when he tried so hard to endure it was with great suffering and pain. At that time, many concerns popped up in his mind, regardless of the embarrassment if he accidentally pees on stage or if he must instantly run out for the toilet amidst the speech, what would happen to his future career if this speech failed etc. On that moment his concentration focuses only on enduring until he cannot carry on with the speech and loses consciousness to the pee which triggered up the subconscious to handle the rush over to the toilet as instinct by notwithstanding loose face or loose character or whatever. By this incident John's subconscious noted it down as a real thread for 'speech = pee' and since then John is always concerned about pee every time he has a speech.

For a viable solution, if we had recognized the pattern of this phobia, we can just alter it, by making him perspire before the speech, the situation will trigger another platform, maybe from flight to fight, then the end result might be different.

One thing that we can be assured of is nothing can be changed if we change nothing.

Chapter 14

SOUND OF THOUGHT

Hey Jack, have you seen Jones recently? Rob asked. "Why did you ask for him just now, we have not seen Jones for several years". Rob was stunned for a while and said that he also had no idea why. It's just that Jones' face pops up indistinctly in his mind.

A few hours later, a car sounded outside the door, and it appeared to be the " long time no see" Jones! Could it be that Rob got some source of signal from Jones when Jones thought of visiting him?

Also, on a trip to the South, Helen happened to sing one very old song that nobody hears nowadays. However, there won't be question If it's not the case that Rose also lingering humming this song deep in her mind once she saw the place that she used to be in the past while this song was on the chart.

The problem is what inspired Helen to sing this song since she has no any background on the place. Once being questioned the answer is 'she doesn't know', just instantly willing to sing and that's it.

Now let's come behind the scene and see what happened in the case of this mysterious signal, where is it from. If the thought has sound there should be no problem since both, Rob or Helen can simply hear it and that's all. But in fact, does thought indeed has sound and can it be sent over distant, this should be the right question. However, if we can prove that thought really has sound and it can be heard even in a distant, then problem solved.

Ok, let's move over to see how thought generates sound. By this time there shouldn't be any disputes or arguments on electric nature of brain signal, since we can buy the proof like 'Emotiv' (brain reader) at around US$800 only, through https://www.emotiv.com/ and see how it work at https://youtu.be/8Hyhljnq9Z4 or https://youtu.be/Czsr_2IE7Aw or how EEG (Brain Signal Reader) work at https://youtu.be/8a5X5ABgBnU.

Since brain signal is confirmed to be electro activities which generate electromagnetic field on its flow, frequency and wavelength should be there. Both characterize the electromagnetic field and that is the so-called thought's sound which we try to figure it out on this chapter.

After knowing on how thought sounded, the next step is knowing how one can hear it.

The capability of human being on capturing information not

only through hearing, we have 5 sense organs which is the eyes, ears, nose, tongue, and skin to capture signal of light, sound, smell, taste, and touch. Besides that, there's still the existence of 6th sense that vaguely flips up on some unintentional occasion which we normally, named it as 'Instinct' on a low-level live platform, or 'Perception' on a high level. This 6th sense indeed is not mental or spiritual substance that is intangible or single physical organ that still on sci-fi mysterious version, but it is a system or sensing function under the subconscious division, co-existing and working between 5 organs and those memory agglomerates on each and every cell, whether on the eyes, ears, nose, tongue skin or brain. Once the source of signals like thought-wave or thought-frequency has passed through these existing 5 sense channels and process together with all memories concerned, it draws up an interpretation then give us the perception.

For the abilities or level of how one can capture the signal or how they can accurately interpret the information, it depends on many factors like how they developed their senses, how strong the signal is, how much weight of memory concerned on those signals being agglomerated through each very being's lifetime experiences and the ability to simulate the situation.

In the case of Rob, Jones is his very close friend, they lived together for over 10 years. Rob knew Jones in all aspects no matter what he loves, what he likes, what he doesn't like or what he hates. Rob always can guess how Jones feels, what he thinks or what he going to say, that means, Rob has tons of memory about Jones on his storage on every single cell concerned, that makes it easier to access Jones. Once Rob gets even a bit of thought wave from Jones's intention of planning to visit him. And as we know, frequency or radio frequency can travel on very long distance.

For Helen, she didn't have much info about Rose, but she had the bulk of memory on the song, hence just a bit of melody frequency can easily trigger up the song. For example, if I am humming on my mind like 'It's been a long day….', I thought all of you know what song I'm singing.

Chapter 15

DISREGARD THE CLOSE

Jim's brother studied and lived in the UK since 1980. He never takes care of his parents since then. However, every time he comes back and spends his holiday here, Jim's mum would give special care to him in the manner that Jim, who served her for more than 40 years, never get such an impressive care from her. Jim always had this question in mind is this unfair deal normal for all people. And yes, it is, people always disregard the close.

The purpose of this story is so simple, it's a matter of ignorance. Since what mum gets from Jim was repeated for a long time until it became a predictable experience, at that moment the subconscious took it as normal, hence bypassed the "evaluation of value' of the consciousness which exist mostly for novels. That's means everything Jim did after that never crossed the threshold of acknowledgment of her subconscious until it is aroused by her interest in any other event.

However, for Jim's brother, his care for his mum was constant through the constant rate of care for her was very low, thus she will always recognize his goodness while ignoring that of Jim's.

This also can explain the lover who received very good care during the first stage and indifferent later. Hope always laid on a novel.

For solution if one doesn't want to be ignored, just move in and move out from time to time, then they will become novel all the times.

Chapter 16

SICKNESS ACCORDING TO INFORMATION

Allan felt uncomfortable this morning, he had few sniffs and some sign of fever. But the overall appearance was still good. On the way to his office, he took a visit to a nearby hospital with the intention to get some medicines. But as he is being informed by the doctor that he may be subjected to quarantine as it possible that he is infected with Dengue.

After he was admitted and changed his dress to a hospital apparel, the overall appearance of Allan seems to grow worse, he was pale, his eyes were red, and looked severely sore. Many friends visited him at noon and try to soothe him with encouraging words that there should be nothing grave with your body, dengue is not a big deal these days, current technology can handle it at ease. However, the encouragement had little to comfort Allan, he was still nervous like that for the whole day until next morning when the doctor paid a visit and informed him Of the result that he only had a simple cold. By hearing this he became fresh and strong as usual in an instant. By this case, it's clear that Allan's health relied not only on the symptom itself but also on the information he got.

Indeed, pain or illness doesn't come directly from disease, but it is reacting of our subconscious in term of warning sensation to the brain about some type of stimulated trigger giving signals that there may be a threat to our survival. And the said stimulant may either be an invasion of a real disease knowing from immune system or information on disease detected from an external source. In this case, Allan got information from the doctor which he accepted as a reliable source that made his subconscious reacted and made it pale to secure energy for the heart on the first stage, then follow with another necessary measure on energy preservation whichever fit for himself based on his lifestyle.

However, this will not happen to the one who always meditates since they can release most of the illusive frightening signal before it can trigger up the subconscious to react and we can see more details of 'Meditation' on Part 3 of Life Editing.

Chapter 17

PREMONITION

Alex and Pam looked so happy because of the new apartment that they decided to move in quickly. They looked at this place for close to 3-4 times. Both were greatly satisfied with this apartment, it's a lively, bright and vivid home. However, upon Alex handing over his cheque to the apartment's owner for payment, the room's environment suddenly changed. It became dark, gloomy and depressing. Alex didn't know why, but after getting back home he could feel something bad running after this deal. This feeling did terrify him a lot till Alex had to discuss with Pam on disposing of the deal. However, after discussion, they both agreed to sell it out after a legal transfer. But just a few days after that Alex lost Pam in a car accident before he could sell it out as intended.

Enigma being concealed is where Alex get those signals of premonition. In this case, it is not the sound of thought as we used to describe, but it is the sound, sequel from their deed which we shall dig deep in details on Part 2 of Life science.

Before the coming of a big wave, a small signal normally arrives first and that is the case of this enigma.

52

Chapter 18

HEART-BROKEN

Lily is pretty and alluring, but she nearly lost her life last month by suicide since she found out that her boyfriend betrayed her. In her mind, she thought that there could be no one in this world that could replace him.

Isn't it true that Lily cannot find a new appropriate one out of the millions after the shock of betrayal? This answer should be known to all normal people, who aren't on a 'Heartbroken' state, that it's not true. After one being overwhelmed by the grief of disappointment for a while, they will recover and be able to have a new relationship with someone again which we have seen evidence in this kind of situation all the times. If this is the case, why should be suffering once they depart or lose their love? Why must they be grief-stricken so much?

Love can be counted as an asset once officially agreed on both sides. its status won't differ much from the contract but will be harder or weaker in bond depending on the period of duration. The long duration relates to the agglomeration of more memory, thus the subconscious will register it as part of life especially for the one who relies on another party, if they pretend to lose it, subconscious will direct body's 'Primal System' to stimulus pain for push on doing something to take him or her back. However, this can persist for sometimes, once time passed and that memory cell died off (our cell naturally die and replace every day), the matter will become better and they may be able to start a new life again as long as they do not wallow in such thoughts repeatedly.

And even so, we have always heard that time is the best healer.

Chapter 19

NO ONE

Tom worked alone for his family while his wife to absolute responsibility for their 3 kids. Family's direction always relied on Tom decision, until the day that those kids grew up and had their own will. Tom's decision was being challenged from time to time while his wife always supported the kids. Finally, the family's unity and wellness were affected due to the constant hazzle and squabbles with Tom's decisions. Tom's wife and children moved out of the house, and he stayed alone for 10 years ever since.

From that incident Tom's personality changed, he suffered from insomnia and depression, thus needed psychotherapy from time to time. If one had the opportunity to converse with him, one will find out that his deep bitterness would always emerge from his conversational phrase such as:,whatever "I don't care", "I'm alone, "I've no one", "I don't need to give a damn to anyone..." or "Nobody cares about me, why do I have to care for someone...". Each word of his expresses his deep coldness and loneliness.

Tom perception of 'since nobody cares about him why does he have to care for others' put him on this state of misery. Only if he opens his mind and investigate the real situation, he will discover that the problem happened from his persistence and pestering thought of his past. Why he doesn't know such an easy solution of 10 years loneliness. Is it worth being like this? If we care for nobody, who will care for us.

Unfortunately, Tom's subconscious had repeatedly learned only to take revenge for the challenge until it left no room for another choice of release and relaxation. This is the power of repeated actions which we will see more in details in the next chapter.

Chapter 20

JUST HAS TO WORK

Matt is my former director. His performance was quite outstanding. Also, his family is wealthy, his asset is more than enough for the rest of his life. we used to discuss what life should be after retirement. He told me his plan on how he would spend the whole day on golfing and traveling. I told him that he is not a golfer, his career field is here in business, his passion is an achievement in this field, he repeated it for more than 30 years, hence, it's not possible for him to just live with no achievement, especially for himself who others must look up to. He said that this may be possible for others but not for him since he loves golfing and traveling more than anything else and he always dreamt of the great days after retirement which would come in the next few years. It will be the time that he would take a rest, then give himself a reward for all these years of hard work.

Two years after his retirement, I heard that he's back to work somewhere as a Managing Director. When I had the chance to converse with him, he accepted that what I told him was right. After a few years of self-reward, it was boring of how time elapsed day by day without any value, he started seeking for the meaning of life which he doesn't know exactly what it is. It's neither money nor achievement as he already possessed all that. However, he feels better once he's back to work and looking for next retirement to reward himself again like a slave that is not willing to leave cause he doesn't know where to go exactly.

This case of Matt is like George case, which we going to learn more in details on next chapter, but still not deep down to the terrible loop. Once he found out that he was not great in golfing and cannot produce great income or achievement from traveling, he decided to turn back to work and find new achievement to answer the subconscious question of 'what we are living for', otherwise death will flip up since there are no any other goals.

Chapter 21

AUDITOR'S INSTINCT

Tim is a normal office worker. His job was periodically audited from time to time on the annual schedule. Tim was always excited once he's faced with auditors no matter if he has some problems or not. However, the thing that made him startled all these time round is that once there were some mistakes concealed, Tim would pray round and round for Auditors not to keep an eye on it, but unfortunately, it looks like all auditors have some special spiritual strength to read his mind. If there was no problem, they wouldn't check seriously, but if there was, they always keep straight to the concealed one as if they have their own Radar then end up with CAR (Corrective Action Request). In this case, should it be possible that Auditors had the extra spiritual strength to look through Tim's mind, or they just have some mental practice until they can hear people's thought? Maybe even Auditors themselves doesn't know.

Cases like this do not only happen on Audit Career, both police or investigator are included. They just look around and they can find the suspect, but unfortunately such kind of instinct cannot be used in court, otherwise, all despicable guys may be put in jail day by day until it remains only the good guys.

Skillful police may have sensed a perpetrator if we have some smugglings on our immigration, they will sense it even with our indifferent faces and normal breath because they have long developed on how thought signal of the perpetrators looks until it was noted down on their subconscious. Only a tiny source of the signal being captured, they can easily match with their long weight memory and catch up. ., like Shazam Apps on mobile phone which can Identify the media playing around us with just a tiny bit of melodies captured.

An experienced auditor also senses the case, if we have some little-hidden agenda which we do not want them to find out, they always be there.

From this event, there is a clue for the idea that strong emotion like hatred, passionate, rage, frightening, fear, lust, greedy or any strong desire can generate strong signals that may be able to benefit one who experiences some sense on it like good wife, also the best example, in this case, she always has sense once we did some mysterious things.

Girls also have sense once there was someone looking at her beast, though they were beyond her eyes sight.

Chapter 22

LIGHT-SPEED CALCULATION

If we drive a car straight forward and see some people pretending to cross the road. For normal calculation, we would simply take 'distance' divided by 'speed' for both people and car to find out time matched on estimated hit point. If not match, we just simply move pass. But if timing to the hit spot from calculation is overlapped, next option will be looking at driver's side mirror to see if there is another car on our side, then dodge, if there is none, or calculate access time between people, our car and other car, if there is one following on our side.

Math problem for the latter will be simulated between rush up and keep straight pass or dodge people then overtake the followed car, if there should have some gap left, or stop in place doing nothing, or just slow down and let all events cleared up first.

All these problems are certainly mathematical problems which normally need big concentration while calculating. Thus, for the one who is just new to driving, their solution will just simply stop with no calculation since it's too complicated for limit time, but for the experienced ones, simulation like this is common even if they're on converse with someone over the phone, and driving with one hand, they still can drive through slippery with right decision, if there is no other unexpected event intervene.

Why can this happen? what is the difference between a newbie and experienced? Is experienced brain really that fast and if it so, why is that experienced drivers don't have the same speed on math exam? The reason behind this is our subconscious drive it by 'Photo recognition' accumulated from time to time, no calculation made, like fingerprint matching on phones Once scenario matched, decision done. Before photo recognition, there're still some steps, firstly we have 'Learning', 'Trial and Error', 'Lesson Learned' and 'Knowledge Know-how', all these gatherings done by 'Conscious', and the next steps of 'Experience', 'Skill' and 'Instinct' carried on by 'Subconscious'.

On 'Instinct' stage subconscious will direct everything effectively and accurately on their own and hard for us, as conscious, to step in easily. That's why once we get angry we can't easily step in to break, or once we are scared of ghost, we cannot stop it even if we know that it's not true since we have plenty of photo recognition on how ghost looks like, repeated from stories or movies, till it becomes our instinct already.

This case of driving also the same, if we try to step in, our skill will drop and error can easily happen since there are two systems reluctantly scheduling on same operation while conscious need time for calculation, but subconscious want to follow photo recognition, that's why accident can always happen once there are some unexpected intervention on the way for new driver, but not certain for the experienced one, since they may still have another photo recognition on such a case too.

By this service of the subconscious, we may call it Autopilot, Automation, Autorun, Reflector Instinct. Besides, it helps us handle most of the things, it also creates a problem for us as well. There are many problems that we already referred to in previous topics.

To manage our subconscious on the correct track, we need to verify what exactly is best for our life, then cultivate it up accordingly. We will see more in details on how to cultivate it correctly on Part 3 of 'Life editing'

Chapter 23

CANCER, THE MIGHT OF REPEATITION

Why the wheel of fortune jackpot to someone to have cancer as a lucky draw while so many people don't even have little chance to experience it. Cancer is randomly fallen on someone or not, and what it is.

Cancer was indeed occurred by the power of repeatation not lucky draw. On the early stage of guitar practice, our fingertip will pain from the repeated pressing of the strings but after a while, the cell on fingertip will be agglomerated to be bumper to support the press. Subconscious will direct the body function not to dispose dead cell on fingertip as it normally did but will keep it in place as bumper instead since pain is one factor of survival concerned and the subconscious main task is survival.

Cancer is also the same as a fingertip on a guitar string. By our environment or lifestyle, we repeated something that effect some survival concerned on internal organ no matter if it is smoking that irritated bronchial or lung, eating some food that irritated intestine, regular breathing of carbon or any toxins that mix with blood flow then agglomerated leucocyte to cover it until those cells are thick, overburdened liver by alcoholic overwhelming, always stressed by work, family affairs, rage, grieve, greed, fear or any other frightening emotions, was also the case since it keeps on shocking brain cells, heart squeeze, raise up blood pressure all the times until subconscious find it necessary to intensify the cell on that area for the sake of repeated pain.

Besides those main causes of cancer, there're still numerous factors that can create internal cell agglomerated which leads to cancer, however its root cause all originated from repeat and pain. Thick outside like guitar case, we can just remove it off, but thick inside is elusive. First, there is no room inside available to extend, every organ was fixed, no space left. Once some become thicker, it is unavoidable to huddle, scramble or struggling on others and led to inflammation if it was long-lasting. Once subconscious recognizes it as long-term pain, a solution of cell agglomerated will be permanent and this is what we call 'Cancer'. To eliminate it, we must remove it off too, but through surgery through irradiation or chemotherapy. However, just removing the agglomerated cells, don't cleanse all cancer causes, since those agglomerating command from subconscious being diffused through all nearby cells, but to what extent nobody knows exactly, that's why we must do cancer therapy through certain extra areas to kill or permanently erase all existing command. Only one cell with this special command left, cell proliferate system will copy it up again and again than become cancer again. And this is how vicious and elusive it is.

Besides sudden cure, we still have an optional natural way to cure cancer, that's also the evolutionary capability of the subconscious as the best person to catch a thief is another thief.

If we change all environment and lifestyle including eating, subconscious may evolve to another direction and cease to trigger proliferate of cancer cells, since there are no further threats as it is on those areas and let it fade out according to normal cell proliferation until it ceases to exist. Therefore, some people in the city who move to urban and change to be vegetarians with new lifestyle can recover from cancer, while someone in urban who is vegetarian from the beginning still has cancer persisted on since it occurred under those situations and there is no change.

It's extremely hard to find out what we took in the effect that trigger subconscious to produce cancer cell since we took in numerous things including emotion. To totally change the way of living, a chance to jackpot from change is always high.

Chapter 24

GET-LOSS VS GIVE-RECEIVE

Why is someone destined to fight for everything, but some just sit and all fortunes drop on their head.

In fact, Get or Receive doesn't differ in terms of physical gain as we indeed gain something, but to Get we need to put effort or force to fight for it, while Receive we put nothing or we may claim that it comes on 'Free'. Hence Receive is more favorable to the subconscious in terms of survival quest than getting because Receiving has no energy usage.

Loss and Give are also on the same track since both lost something in physical terms but Give is happier to subconscious since this kind of loss is on purpose, no matter 'for love, for sympathy, for respect, for social acceptance or for being good guy', it's kind of willingly or voluntary while loss was involuntary.

Receive is flashback reaction from giving since we put effort or force on ourselves to release our belongings to others according to the law of 'Action and Reaction' or 'What goes around comes around,' while Loss is a flashback of getting since we put force to fight on others. And the loss is not something that our subconscious is willing to accept, we need to fight back as it is involuntary since we lose something that we used to put energy to Get it. Thus, Get and Loss, both brought back unhappiness to the subconscious in terms of survival quest since both loss energy, while Giving and Receiving reflects happiness since only one energy is lossed on Giving but voluntarily.

Get gains joy, while Give gains happiness. If we know this sequela of the deed, we are free to choose what type of fate we wish. Both are the same, but for sake of subconscious, it is totally different. The point is most of us don't know or not believe in the law of Action that makes most people made the wrong choice and face with unwilling fate.

Chapter 25

HIGH DEMAND LESS CHOICE

Wills gave all the best to his son all these years, with great love regardless of the best school, best car, best meal, best resident and best service from all his subordinates by ignoring that this good intention is equaled to putting his kid in jail on top of the triangle where there is no much choice for him to choose.

If we divided the triangle into 3 parts horizontally, and put our kids on the top frame, their basic simple living will be on a top tier where most people move on. Thus, dream or hope that others hang on becomes nothing for them, then what will be their dream or hope? Maybe it's the best of the best on top of the triangle, but that point needs to compete to death since there are not over 100 places out of millions of millions. If your kid was cultivated from a triangle base through the top, their knowledge, experience, skill, and intellect may surpass others and win the top then reach the hope. Unfortunately, they're not the least like us who fight all the way from base to top, cause they are being put on top from the beginning, where they can have all those competition qualifications. Also, their immunity to suffering, pain or ridicule is minimal, how can they endure all obstacles of fear, disappointment or miss fortune coming from the flashback of their arrogance? Resource to fight may be given through high education but immune to trouble and endure needed agglomerate, no ultimate shortcut.

Hence, putting them in comfort equals putting them in a hopeless jail. If there are some days of loneliness, boredom, and awakening, they will face them with extreme grieve, questions of 'What they are living for'.

Chapter 26

PRECOGNITION

While the car was halted on a red traffic light at Radisson Square's intersect, Sam happened to scream out loud as if some upheaval instantly emerged right in front of his car, while another 3 persons in the car sensed nothing. But just 2-3 seconds from such precognition of Sam, 'Bang' sounded from the opposite lane, a car shot over another on a severe car crash.

Initially, Sam thought that he had the superpower of precognition since he always took meditation practice on daily bases, but the question was how short it was, his precognition popup only 2-3 seconds before the incident.

Anyways, after spending more times on contemplation, Sam had learned that it was not the so-called mysterious precognition, but it was again the sound of thought like auditor's case that is being described on the previous chapter.

Sam sensed the sound of the frightening signal in the brain of those car drivers that just emerged in a blink before his car rushed

into the crash. This could happen, though Sam had no strong
repeated database on this kind of signal in his memory, because
the signal of thought waves that emitted out was quite a strong
combination with Sam's skill on sensing through his long-term
practice on meditation hence, Sam could catch up the particle of
those car drivers thought nearly on the same second.

Chapter 27

COMPENSATION

Jacob suffered for a very long time from Heel Pain or Plantar Fasciitis while physical therapy cannot permanently recover him from this pain. Jacob already tried every method to cure it, but nothing better until one day he found by himself that it was caused by his abnormal walking posture, that is tiptoe walking which originally caused by his knee pain in form of compensation. By the way, after knee pain being removed by PT, Jacob still didn't change the tiptoe walking, it evolved to be normal posture by the subconscious, and that is the case why no PT can initiate his evolution back to normal again.

In such case, Jacob needs to start righteous walking practice up to the same period equal to what he wasted on tiptoe walking to stimulate or cultivate the righteous walking posture, back to recover from heel pain but not exactly to normal since there is crack bone already existed there from long time tense on plantar.

Besides this plantar, there are still many cases referred to this concept where only some pro-PT can find out this kind of pain effected from compensation, from their very long-term experiences.

Chapter 28

FEAR OF DEATH

Ford worked in a well-established company. He was a middle management with acceptable performance. His salary, house, car, insurance, investment or saving could afford him to live in comfort even after retirement. Unfortunately, everyone who knew Ford noted that he believes in the power of money, he never relaxes on finance, no matter the situation. If someone asked him why he was so strict to himself on such a hard saving, he would explain logically that if you don't save from today, that you still have might to do so, once something happens in the future, you will have no fund to pay for hospital fee at the end.

Ford lived up to 70 years of age, he spent more than 3 years in ICU at the end of his life and it was true that his whole life saving can support him up to 3 years in five stars hospital, but in Zombie state with Feeding Tube hanged on, Oxygen Pump in, Breathing Tube inserted, and Chase Tube drained out, since he cannot walk, eat, breath or excreted by himself.

It's rather cruel on this day that money can really buy everything even death. The hospital can keep our lives with all life supports if we still have money to pay. Then who dare says, let the patient leave in peace if they still have money on hand to extend. Such is the case of many families, they suffered from paying hospital fee till they were exhausted with death as the final result.

Often, the wealthier the person was, the more they feared death. Ford was like this. He has held enough wealth that caused him to have an enormous love for life and an enormous fear of death. When he was pushed up to the edge, his desire to live was terrible; what sort of things wouldn't he do? How many people were there that were able to face death without fear? Most people, when facing their impending doom, bet everything they had to fight for even slimmest chance of survival. At that time, thing like dignity, honor and wealth all becomes a joke. Ford agreed to pay all his reserve to the hospital as planned hence, carried all pains on his last 3 years in ICU to stay for a little longer.

I don't think there would be someone jealous on this kind of longtime ICU experiences. However, to face death with less fear, and not be along on Ford's path was easier said than done, one may need long-term meditation to create natural intuition towards death to soften strength of their survival direction in subconscious for not struggling overboard as Ford did which we will show the way on Part 3 of 'Life Editing'.

Chapter 29

DEPRESSION

George is wealthy, he has a good job, good achievement in life. He has nearly everything that common people dream of. One day, I met him sitting in front of his mansion in a dark and gloomy expression.

"What's wrong with you"? I asked, unceremoniously. George revealed some inner feelings of grieve, dispirit, distraction and depression with reasons unknown. According to what he told me, it just happened recently. He felt no happiness on TV broadcast, Movie, Chit-Chat, Gameplay or any entertainments including Investment News, and even Profit or business achievement info that he's most excited about. Once this mode of gloomy catches up with him, wealth becomes nothing. Money or pride can't cheer up his mental status as it used to be. He lost interest in all activities he once enjoyed, he became bored with everything and lost target of living. He really didn't know what he lived for and what would be after this lifespan, they still have 'HIM' or not. He's deeply afraid of what he doesn't know.

Not only George, in fact, most people always have this feeling in dark corners of their minds, the similar questions of what we are living for, what is life, who are we, we work for what, what will be us after this life since the destination of all is death? Such a question is lingering around most people all the times. It's pestered and agitating within us, waiting for the chance to churn up on loneliness, especially for the one who seldom has chance to be alone e.g. Super Star, Wealthy, Noble or any Top Tier Persons because all these people have very low resistance to loneliness. Once one touches this taboo of thought, their willpower will tremble in cold and fluctuate to scary extend then needs to retreat in an instant, otherwise, they will tend to be locked into 'Depression' symptom as this case of George. And we may refer all these scary questions as 'Black Hole of Mind'.

Now let's see Depression in Physic way, according to Psychology or Physiology, depression is the state of mental illness with effect by Biochemical of Neurotransmitter especially Serotonin which is the most outstanding on active or happiness concerned. Hence Serotonin depletion in thebrain may lead to grieve, sadness, anxiety or worthlessness. Currently, depression can be treated by medication like antidepressants which is SSRI (Selective Serotonin Reuptake Inhibitors), for example. SSRI will go to inhibit the reuptake of Serotonin in the brain and make it sufficient to normal usage which in turn will return happiness to us. However, by sending in the inhibitor to inhibit, it's not actually the way to solve problems permanently if we still don't know the root causes of what originated depletion of Serotonin or over reuptake of Serotonin. If the root cause is still there, some days it may trigger back again. Also, by using of antidepressants, there is a side effect of overactive if we do not stop in the appro-priated period. For more information about SSRI, you may visit https://youtu.be/3c-KTc923Bc.

Back to the point of this book, our interest is not exactly on physic or biochemical mechanism since we are concerned only on the elusive subconscious. Let's see how subconscious relates to serotonin, depletion, and depression. As we have already talked a lot on previous pages about survival which is supposed to be a core function of the subconscious. Anything that will affect survival, subconscious must take caution and find the way to solve it. The only direction that exists in the subconscious is that we (our body) must survive no matter what. However, if someone touches the above taboo of 'Black hole in mind' which seriously is against 'Survival Will' since it was the problem of death concerned, subconscious will scare to dead and try all out to solve the problem by even wrapping up energy in order to prolong energy usage for lifespan extension, and this process includes Serotonin Depletion which supposed to be the main factor of depression, since Serotonin concerns energy usage for active purpose. We may compare this effort to one trying to survive the disaster, what they will do is to preserve food, water, etc. for survival too.

The way the subconscious handles problem is always straight-forward, lack of energy means death. Hence energy preservation should be considered as an appropriate measure. The Subconscious knows only how to direct body function but it doesn't know much on whatever reasons or side effect involved while conscious knows everything but has no right to direct control over the body. The only way to manipulate our subconscious to direct body on track is to educate them which we shall go deep in details on Part 3 of 'Life Editing'.

In this case, conscious thinks about the problem and the subconscious acts on its own measure, which in turn isn't the exact way we are pleased since we become depressed instead.

Now back to the problem of 'in which condition did people trigger up those taboo questions? There are so many situations concerned, such as chronic illness, hopelessness, so lazy to handle low value job, boring of work, not happy with workmate, feeling of desolatation, loneliness, not meeting target, discouragement, strong disappointment, sadness of incapability, grieve with love epic, upset with everything, feeling worthless, always relying on others and afraid of no one for us to rely on, lack of value and whatsoever fears. All these things can ignite the thought and lead to depression finally.

Fame or power may help boost serotonin for joy, anxiety, pride, and anticipation but it's subject to people's response. If there is no one to praise or accept, it will be worse since these type of people who has fame or power especially the one at the peak, are less immune to loneliness and will be caught up by depression more easily. That's why some of this group needed to put all their efforts to maintain the position since next to peak is 'Down'.

On the other hand, if worthiness or hope is still there, problems shouldn't be obvious, life can move ahead, target by target. Hence people with hope are always immune to depression since they still know 'what they are living for'. New Hope, a new awareness is also the same. If one does not isolate themselves, they still can recognize that life can go on purposefully, there are still many novels to learn and acknowledge, many new experiences and new environment waiting for them out there. That's why some people need some trips sometimes to fresh up their life.

To emerge from depression if it is the case, besides antidepressants, time is the main key, if there was no repeat, since memory cell die every day which represented the word 'bury' or 'forget'.

In George case to avoid a repeat, he must have crossed over medication or treatment of antidepressant and back to temporary liveliness first, then exit from his normal environment, maybe on poorer status and await new hope of others instead of self-care, find new struggles, new achievement of the others, help them and be happy with them. At that time, his mental state may be improved to another direction of living for others, then exit from the loop to liveliness again.

Men that are afraid of death or non-existence is the fact, but someone can die for the King, die for Nation, fight for freedom, fight for family, fight for their love etc. Hence one who has love in others will not be subject to depression since worthiness of living still exists forever and the question of 'what we're living for' will have no chance to pop up at ease.

In the past, depression was seldom found because people are

not being put in frame like working from 8.00 to 17.00 or being controlled under the vicious rule which adds up day by day, while pressure and competition becomes more intense and trust being left behind since each being must struggle to be outstanding for their achievement and pay. People become tenser on self-orientation, more selfish and isolated which is the starting point of stress and loneliness.

In the old days, lifestyle was not like this, people worked on free will, competition wasn't much, they live together, helped each other, their social life was real not online stuff, there was no much secret to be kept or lies for any benefits, then there was no problem of trust, no isolation and no question of 'what we're living for'. Also, they all had faith in Dhamma, in God or in any holy sacred that they rely on, then there was no problem of life beyond death. Unlike people of this day who believe on their own might, ability, and intelligence. Once they collapse from the inside, there is no external faith to rely on, like a perfect swimmer on the vast sea where no shore to be seen.

Chapter 30

FATE: WHAT GOES AROUND, COMES AROUND

Stefan is a wise and logical man, he believes in hard work, hard work pays more than a happy life. He always talks to others that man must fight for their own glory. Good deeds, the good life is the matter of nonsense, no reasons, no logic. Immediately I asked him if someone worked so hard and achieved his glory as he said, then his being cut off in a car accident, how could he explain this. Stefan just responded that, if that was the case, it is 'Fate'. I startled for a moment and asked him why he just lifted the word 'Fate', what is the logic behind this 'Fate'. He as the logical man said that fate is no logic?!?!

A few years later, after Stefan attained his glory, he just fainted and fell with a severe injury on his brain. He could no longer talk or walk, thus tightly spent the whole time on the bed for a year and finally gone. Who knows how FATE works.

Fate, in fact, is destined by deeds according to the third law of Newton which states that 'For every action, there is an equal and opposite reaction'. Such, the case Fate is not concerned with wealthy achievement or glory, it's just the reflection of what we have done consciously or unconsciously, thus people who don't know this logic may create deeds unconsciously by their subconscious which represents habit, attitude or instinct, and face with unpleasant fate or involuntary pain as reflect.

In this case of Stefan, what deed involved on his fate as he was the very tough guy and always asked others to shut up if their conversation was not in accordance with his opinion. Hence most people especially one inferior to him would always be put on grieve by his direct word. This behavior went on for a very long time until it was embedded into his subconscious and became his profound character, thus reflected on an appropriate time when he fell with the result of shutting up himself for the rest of his life.

For the proof of this kind of reflection, we shall dig deep further in details on Part 2 of Life Science.

—— PART 2 ——
LIFE SCIENCE

To understand life, we need to know the structure and functions of the body and cell is Anatomical and Physiological.

To understand life's behavior, we need to know how 'SUBCONSCIOUS' works, that it is Psychological or Information Technology.

To understand life pathway, we need to learn Physic or Dhamma (natural rule of life) which talks about Karma (retribution of action) and Destiny (life path).

For afterlife, we need to know the Reincarnation process.

According to Part 1, we referred that life consist of 3 systems, first is 'Primal System' that run normal life profound function, then 'Conscious' that act as Managing Director who analyses all environment and generate responsive policy, and 'Subconscious' who take policy to operate and convert it to routine operation after certain repeats.

On this part of 'Life Science', we shall not talk much on 'Primal System' since it's not quite complicated and can be studied more from Anatomy and Physiology which already contained enormous in details.

Instead, we shall seriously focus on 'Subconscious' and its sequel since it is big influence over our life, illness, and destiny according to what we have shown in Part 1.

Many times, subconscious force us to do or feel something against our will, regardless of rage, hatred, love, greed, grieve, excitement or fear. Most of their action is beyond our control and we always helplessly let it flow as they wish, thus feel bad afterward, like the case of 'always making noise to the kids on starting of holiday trip and putting the whole trip in chaos instead of fun'. I think, nobody is willing to have such kind of incident on the happy occasion, but it always happened. Why can't we control it, isn't it 'US' who does that? The answer should be 'No' since we never wanted it to be like that. The one who did it was 'The Elusive Subconscious' that we mentioned a lot of its boldness or reckless on Part 1.

Since subconscious is beyond our control, does it mean that our life and destiny is beyond our control too? Indeed, the subconscious is not exactly beyond our control, but control cannot do on spot, like upbringing of the kids, we cannot just command or punish them on the spot to change their attitude, we need to cultivate them precisely, delicately from early stage, then they will grow up on right path. Subconscious, indeed, no different from kids. They are being raised up by us, if we gave them an unconsciously wrong path, non-reasoning or instinct reaction all the times they will grow up wild and if they can fight all the way on their wishes, the fight will always be their option, thus fight fate will certainly be their destiny. That's why so many people said, 'Please leave me alone, I want to stay in peace, I want to rest, why do people always create problems for me', in fact, those people created circle of problems by themselves through the cultivation of their subconscious unconsciously on fighting path, how can peace be claimed for. But for the one that agglomerated their subconscious on fear, they will have destined to depress someday.

Compare our body and mind to a car with autopilot, before reading this book, you may be the just a simple driver who knows nothing about the car, and comfort with its auto service. But after knowing how elusive subconscious could create problems for our lives, you may not extremely trust on its performance further and may be willing to pay more attention to how it works and how to maintain, manifest, cultivate or manipulate them in good order that will bring back our righteous and independent.

Computer needs configuration, plane's autopilot needs configuration, the car needs fine tuning, life's autopilot (subconscious) also needs fine tuning too. If we set it right, life will run smooth, if we set it hard, life will fit for fight, if it's weak setting, life is set on fear and if we set it wrong then disaster can be expected.

However, before we can configure or tune-up, we need to have a profound knowledge of how it works first.

Lives system is extremely complicated, though we try to compare to a car, it's totally different from heaven and earth. It's too complicated than computer setup and even worse to recovery systems after virus infiltrated through numerous installation of garbage applications that we think good for our lives on each spot by notwithstanding the sequel.

Life starts with the word 'Homeostasis', the official definition is 'the tendency toward a relatively stable equilibrium between interdependent elements, especially as maintained by physiological processes'.

All systems of our body and mind exist for this 'Homeostasis' purpose or we can simply call it 'Survival System'.

For survival, we have three major systems in 'us' working together, which is 'PRIMAL SYSTEM', 'SUBCONSCIOUS' and 'CONSCIOUS' or we may call it 'ID', 'EGO' and 'SUPEREGO' in term of phycology.

The First Primal system is responsible for all body basic function on physiological bases. This covers 10 major areas such as Skeletal, Circulatory, Nervous, Respiratory, Muscular, Digestive, Urinary, Lymphatic, Endocrine and Reproductive system. These superb systems work together in an excellent robotic chain that keeps our body alive If there is no external tamper from Subconscious which is our main regard in this book, life with food feed in without struggling will have very long lifespan which can correlate to 'standby mode' of mobile phone that can stand for over 3 days if there is no call or any form of operation, while some last only within 2 hours if it is on fighting or adventure gameplay.

Before moving through the details of our main discussion (second system of 'Subconscious'), let's talk a little about our third system first. Our third system is 'Conscious'. If 'Primal System' is an operator, 'Subconscious' will be a supervisor and 'Conscious' can be regarded as Management or Trouble Shooter. The supervisor takes direct control over operator while management or troubleshooter simply assigns works or policies over supervisor from time to time, thus subconscious developed this temp policy to the routine solution, after certain repeated works for further auto service.

Good management will follow up or give close monitoring feedback over a supervisor to assure the correct pathway, while comfort managements rely on great experience and capability of supervisors till being tamed by them instead, thus became void on their misleading and be their slaves afterward, then lost power to resist finally.

Hence all information, solutions or decisions made by conscious needs close monitoring on sequel before subconscious, who always keep an eye on our actions, grabs the scene and seize the power of decision from us by turning it to auto assistant which can be referred to as reflect, habit, behavior or instinct that may either be demonic or righteous. The demonic path had always been synonymous with doing whatever one wished, unlike righteous path where there are still many morals and principles one had to follow.

Many people don't like their own habits, they don't want to get rage, they don't want to be coward, they don't want to be so ruthless, but they have no power to resist since it has already been converted to be auto or subconscious solution by repeating it on their own unconscious cultivation caused by not monitoring the sequel of their response closely.

In this book, we are going to strike back for a second chance.

Chapter 31

PHYSIC OF THE SUBCONSCIOUS

From all we've talked about the subconscious up until now, I think that all of us at least vaguely know how the subconscious affects our life.

If you are already happy with just these information and willing to move over on 'how to adjust, fix or manipulate the subconscious to fit our dream life', you may skip this boring scientific part and move ahead to next part of 'LIFE EDITING' directly, no need to waste time around this Part to reconfirm the content of this book, since I already wasted a lot of my lifespan to prove it out all the ways from electronic, physic, bio, chem, psycho, anatomy, physio even through programming.

However, for someone like me who really rely on scientific and not comfortable to just follow the simple path of life's editing, hence willing to have clear picture on where this elusive subconscious that always creates problem for our life is, and what it looks like, how it functions, can we describe or locate it out in physical way, then let's travel through the most complicated system of the world together.

Subconscious is an auto system manipulated, cultivated or agglomerated from learning and memory. The Nature of the subconscious is intangible, incorporeal like Words or Excel that also intangible, but does exist on our computer and operated by electric signals throughout the computer network. Subconscious also operates all over our neural network in form of electrical signals too, but it is electrochemical. If we really insist to figure out where exactly it is, we may defer that it resides on all synapses (a junction between two nerve cells, consisting of a minor gap across which impulses pass by diffusion of a neurotransmitter). Our nerve cells indeed, don't have one wire running throughout the brain and the body, but it's consist of numerous uncountable wires running with a junction between each of them, and on those borders of junction on each nerve pair have codes of subconscious written up by Protein in form of various signal gate stand for what we knew as 'Memory' whether in terms of sensor or response, similar to 'Logic Gates' in computer science which is the profound base of programming.

This protein built up through Amino Acid and Amino Acid built up through RNA and DNA which contains all Gene or set of command that cover every profound base of our body's functionality.

To have a clearer picture we may reluctantly compare DNA to to character A,B,C,D, then Amino is a word formed up from DNA character, and Protein is a sentence, story or all means, composed or edited from Amino Word. And that's it. If you are willing to dig deeper into physiology you can search on the net with 'Protein Synthesis', keyword since it is a very long story with tons of texts and theory.

Chapter 32

LEARNING AND MEMORY

Learning starts with a novel and turns to be a memory by habitation or Sensitization once the response is being fixed for those new novels.

Habituation will cease in response after a series of repeated actions while Sensitization will tense up response once repeated.

For what will be interpreted as Sensitization, it depends on how one views the novel as life-threatening. If subconscious views those novels as unharmed, Habituation will be in process, but if those novels were taken as life-threatening then memory will be Sensitization.

And this Sensitization is where the elusive subconscious messes up our lives if we do not cultivate them well on what should be a real threat or what should be elusive.

Life-threatening is anything that wastes energy, regardless of bodily malfunction or damage that directly affect to the decrease of energy production. Loss of energy, saving assets, whether it is a real asset like a car or other facilities that facilitate life, even reputation, and work, also energy saving concerned as having a job, having money, then having facilities, having a reputation, then having a job, having labor to facilitate life.

Loss of friends, loss of families, loss of a nation, loss of rights or everything start with loss also be counted as life-threatening.

Any novels that may possibly affect all the above factors may be treated as life-threatening depends on, to what decree persons or their subconscious memory base view it from their experience and environment. If their concept is righteous, then most of life-threatening they counted on is a real threat, but for the ignorant most of it is illusion, 80-90% of life threat in normal people is illusions if we refer to Part 1 of this book.

However, many Sensitizations can be turned to be Habituation if we can persistently endure the subconscious stimulus until it overwhelms the life-threatening path, means no further worth for fight, or just being awakened and transcend the illusion or ignorance of life threat, then release and relax the tenses.

And this second method of release and relax is the way of 'LIFE EDITING' that this book was intended to talk about.

Now back to physical of how Signal or Logic Gate of all Learning Habituation or Sensitization being created. Process started from collide of external object, like particle/wave/chemical/ direct contact from seeing/hearing/taste/smell/touch, with receptors on nerve cells of eyes, ear, tongue, nose and skin, then stimulus those cells to generate specific Logic Gate or Memory for each type of contact depends on threshold and saturation of each very being signal, correlate to playing guitar which obviously shows some differences on fingertip at start, but will unveil significantly thick and sensitive to each single guitar chord and string once being repeated to certain limit. More repeat more gate and more memory longevity. This type of memory is what we know as 'Learning and Recognition'.

Besides this learning and recognition, there're also signal gate originated from collide of internal signal or neurotransmitter designated from brain and spinal cord to stimulate some Responsive or Reflex to certain event no matter it is 'Normal Responsive on work', 'Reflex', 'Memory Recall' or 'Alarm from internal organ on irregularity of normal functioning'.

While Responsive is under somatic or voluntary which is under our brain control, Reflex is auto or involuntary which is beyond our brain control.

Reflex consists of routine reflex from viscera communications for normal operation of the body function no matter the breathing, digesting, energy producing, cell repair or cell proliferation and death cell dispose etc. Another type of reflex is special task force beyond routine, where subconscious played its majestic roles by toggle back and forth between Normal or Resting State called Parasympathetic system and Fight or Flight State called Sympathetic system. And our overall problem is here no matter it is behavior habit emotion or even fate.

Subconscious system's nature is a set of signal gates represented functions or command for each very being situation of fight or flight depends on each very beings experience and environment.

This set of specific function gates consist of specific 'Input Phase' through sensory signal gate on synapse where messages received from eyes, ear, tongue, nose, skin and viscera, and specific 'Output Phase' through motor signal gate where command or call to action being sent out to all viscera or muscles on responsive or reflex related to what is being received from sensor of such specific input phase, like electronic circuit. We can correlate this process to computer locked circuit or data system on CD or a hard disk array that lay on disk's track in meaning designated formation for electronic operation according to our solution designed purposes like 'Streetfighter' game that is being designed to reflect players strike in advance.

Game response indeed not computer figure, but it's human or programmer's will that mirrors their way of reflecting in computer code like what they're subconsciously gated down on their nerve junction.

Hence signal gates on all synapses over uncountable nerve cells throughout our body, not only the one that existed in the brain, can be implied to data or program on 'Hard Disk'.

However, Memory or signal gate unlike data or system on a hard disk that once being recorded will stay there through hard disk lifetime if no erase or overwrite, it eventually, not standing eternally. Memory subjected to decay on time flow if no repeat, like not playing guitar for a while then thick bumper on fingertip will be dispersed, that is what we knew as 'Forget' or 'Fadeaway'.

By the way, memory never happened to be a complete loss since it's not limited only on one nerve cell on every single activity. There is an immeasurable number of cells concerned on each event. Once we see snake then shock and run, there are several communications between cells from receiving a signal through numerous rod and cone cells in eyes on seeing, through massive olfactory receptors in the nose on smelling, and maybe through countless auditory hair cells in the ear on hearing some of snake sound vibration. Even all environments of the surrounding regardless of vision sound smell or a touch of muggy which made us recognize that this kind of place possibly has a snake, also counted on.

Signals from all these receptors will be interpreted and converted into electrochemical signal like fingerprint scan then pass through spinal cord for matching on instant response similar to matching of fingerprint, if memories or subconscious code for auto response about snake do exist out there, signal will smoothly flow in through those uncountable gate on spinal cord and direct through trigger another gates of 'Shocking Action' which is certain type of 'Response' on 'Fight or Flight' series of subconscious set of action that we shall talk about in detail further.

Once a 'Shocking Action' is triggered, shocking signals will be flown throughout uncountable muscle cells all over the body to produce shocking appearance and shocking process, regardless of faded face, cold hand, high blood pressure, fast breathing, screaming or even fleet.

While signal from receptor flow in through snake's gate on nerve cell and direct out to trigger shocking gate of the indent muscle cells on this snake responsive process set, there also another signal from snake's gate correspondingly flow through spinal main wire all the ways to brain for delicate matching inside many areas of brain to find out how to do next. In this case, 'Conscious' will take place to analyses everything, based on precise matching with countless memory on the database in the brain, then come out with a solution of 'Fight or Flight' again. We may have seen some scenario like the first fleet then have an inkling that the snake is only a foot in range, and back to fight after.

Once fleet, it was a subconscious auto response and once back, it was a conscious decision after delicate analysis, correlate to a supervisor did first then correspondingly report to a boss or broad for precise decision afterward. And therefore, we always cannot control our emotion or auto response from subconscious since its process is brief and shorter in distance, just signal in and instant out.

Every cell's communication always leaves some clues out there on cell synapse, no matter much or less, no free communication, like guitar playing, the thick bumper will always be there no matter we if can observe it or not. Since this is the case, all processes from receptors to final action have an immeasurable number of communications implanted on cells concerned, if someone willing to erase or going to lose certain memories on accident, they need to completely rub out all signal gates from all communications connected regardless of gates on cone cells, rod cells. olfactory cells, auditory hair cells and the innumerable sequel cells from those receptors through the spinal cord to the brain which indeed is impossible, thus memory can only be damaged in certain areas on accident which may cause fainting or fading but no absolute loss. And if one is willing to rub out on some miserably memories or bad habit segments, what they can do is only let it be rubbed out naturally on time flow couple with no further add up new on repeat protocol, that's why love is hard to set free since one always repeat that love memory.

Chapter 33

FIGHT OR FLIGHT

Do any incoming signals throughout our five sense of organ which consist of the eyes, ears, nose, tongue, or the skin need a brain or conscious response on fight or flight all the time? The answer is 'No' since we cannot response thousands of info in one scenario like being excited seeing a table, chair, door, windows, or curtain lamp every time we see it, that could have been insanity. Only those novel or new stimulus and life-threatening signals need a response.

For a whole life, repeated actions within an environment or unharmed information, our memory will be shift its responses to Habituation which cease to response after certain repeated actions, since uncountable signal gates is already been there on every single nerve cell to support smooth flow in and flow out, hence there are no hinders or thresholds to initiate any new instant response or alter a sequel decision.

Only fresh info or novel which has no previous subconscious gate set on, electrochemical signals will flood and keep it tight outside synapse of each communication linked cells, wave by wave until its electrochemical force overwhelms the threshold of each cell wall, then signal gate will be stimulated specifically to this individual signal frequency, like light on a film that creates photos. This explains how after the overwhelming force allows all these chemical signals floods in and shoot over through spinal cord to each brain area concerned, which is fixed by nerve junction or synapse on each individual function e.g. 'seeing' to occipital lobe at the back of brain area, 'smelling' to frontal lobe, 'hearing' to temporal lobe while touch and taste to parietal lobe (more in details can be searched through 'Brain Area' keyword), for mapping (similar to Google Search regardless of photo or sound search) to sort out what this novel can be categorized into and it was likely life threatening or not, from the accumulated memories, then flood signal sent out from those categories through its native set of responsive gates, where Fight or Flight was pre-designed as main subconscious, direct to designated motor control area in frontal lobe to generate hormonal command and shoot along with blood vessel, that act as carrier, straight to those individual motor cells corresponding to the muscles for action, whether it is a 'Fight or Flight', in one for all format like gossip thats faster than THE FLASH, to create overall output action gates right to the designed solution. And at the same time, the separate hormonal signal will also shoot to the originated receptors to stimulate direct output gate for the next flood in, which will bypass the brain route and shoot out directly to the responsive muscle cells to decide.

Anyway, the command shouldn't be the command if there is no feedback to follow up. This set of command will also create feedback to the signal gates so in response on the action too, that's why we found cells conversing with each other all the times. Whenever no good feedback from final action cells, process will persist by loop in more aggressive like manner, tenses up all muscles, squeezes the heart harder etc., or pick up new responsive category to handle its until its fruitful, even initiate new internal input for evil responsive categories like illusions and lies to build up fear and stimulate the whole system to find its way back to its original desire, which is still waiting for a good feedback in term of chain reaction, it correlates to anyone who plays chess that try every way to achieve their goal. What we do is what we think and what we think is what the system does inside our brain, and invariably the cells are involved. In term of chess, whether we nearly lose or nearly win we witness both the physical and mental effects that are done by designated command. And this is repre-sented how our response system or subconscious worked to push us for its goal.

As the goal is achieved, these sets of the solution will be taken as next time response until it is repeated and repeated and until nothing affect life, furthermore it becomes a habituation, however, if it's subjected to sensitizations, this auto response will still be there until a threat being solved.

For the category of pre-designed solution or response on novel, if we are fighter, signal flow will map out fight category for trial and error, then signal will be shifted to Fight option, and if the solution worked well in that situation, subconscious code is settled there on all related cells ready for next time automation. And if situation repeated from time to time with achieve weight confirmed higher than fail, this solution gates will be placed on top of the hierarchy for the first choice of reacting, reflex or response. If the failure rate is higher, the next category will be picked up until the system finds the best fit.

By the way, all problems never have only one solution, but the more repeated sequence will have more memory implanted on synapse, then more signal gate imprinted according to the weight of results. In such a case, top of hierarchy or popular gate will always be choice correlate to flooded water into the closed room with numerous groups of drain gate designated to each individual group of action, major water volume will certainly rush through the section with highest drain gate members. And this is where subconscious operation fast track pattern starts on direct control over our Autonomic Nervous System (more physio definition can be searched from the internet with ANS keyword).

This term of ANS may shock your brain caused by complication, thus you may just skip it and keep note only that whatever repeated action or response will turn to be experience, knowledge, skill, habit then instinct step by step depends on the degree of repetition. And each of these steps will help us lighten our brain work. It's autopilot that helps pilot running the plane smoother in normal circumstances.

We must accept that without this help we cannot keep on working the whole day every day with our brain thinking on all events. There are numerous works done by skill unconsciously regardless of driving, singing, sewing, cooking or playing sport etc., even fighting also included. Anyway, each repetitive action also means tougher on withdrawal. Once automation becomes instinct, we nearly have no chance to switch back the control, and that is worse since boss role being shifted from conscious to the subconscious. Thus, we shall lose our human consciousness profile.

Now we may conclude that all human pains come from the mischief of their subconscious on ignorance of how it works. We let them go wild on fight or flight all the times with no good plan on cultivating good memory for a happy life path. Hence, we always face involuntary fate.

Great troubleshooter, however, no match to the good planner.

Chapter 34

FATE AND DESTINY

Fate is in fact destined by deeds according to the third law of Newton which stated that 'For every action, there is an equal and opposite reaction'.

People get what they do or 'What goes around, comes around', it's the effect of their behavior or their Subconscious responded faster beyond their control or awareness since it is an autoflow according to the solution gate as what we have already talked about on the last chapter. Hence most of them don't know why their life will be like this and who controls their destiny.

Firstly, let's proof this theory of reaction in a simple analogy by assuming that a car is a world. If a fly float is in the closed car that ran at speed of 60 miles per hour, how come it didn't flow back and hit the back glass. By the way, even it wants to move back it must fly on its own force. Matter happened like this because there is no empty space within the car. There is an air-filled around on every molecule and this air pressure that fixed the fly on a certain location. If they want to move they need to swim through the air.

Beside the fly in the car, playing badminton on ship desk also is the case. Once the ship moves forward while we hit shuttlecock to the back, shuttlecock indeed must fall on the sea, however, it doesn't have to be like that, we can still play as usual, if a ship sails at a normal speed and surrounding atmosphere is common. The reason is like the fly in the car, since there is no empty spatial on the ship deck, shuttlecock fly by our hit force appropriated to normal pressure of the air surround there as we have been under this pressure or this environment since born. All our functions no matter our mass, activities or force usage being adjusted to this circumstance from early in our life and develop through time until our subconscious knows how to release appropriated force on hit.

Now let's move this analysis to a bigger picture of the world. The World is spherical in shape, we as human being stand on this sphere but never fall out to somewhere, the reason is also the same as we have discussed, we are being packed by surrounding air pressure fit for us or we are born to fit for it, from our evolution through times. And to make a clearer picture of how we are fixed to earth by pressure, let's assume space as white fabric that's being stretched tightly with some ants as figures (representing human being) roaming around the center of fabric, then we place a heavy steel ball (represented earth) on a fabric surface among the ants, what would happen. Ants will be fixed to the surface of steel ball by the pressure of fabric surface against steel ball while having ants in between, but ants didn't die if they born in such circumstance and accustomed with it from the beginning. However, if we replace more weight or lighter weight on, ants will feel different as they can jump high on lighter and may be squeezed to death on heavier like what will affect us on the moon (lighter) or Jupiter (heavier).

Hence, no spatial surrounding us is being confirmed through all above statement, if we initiated some force out there, they should certainly have some force flashback on us in replace like we charged in the room that filled with people till no space left, there should be one guy being chased out of the room.

Therefore, any actions, behavior, thoughts or feelings toward something will certainly reflect but doesn't back on as first come first served, the strong force will back first, that's why we could not match up what result coming from what action. And more worse since we launched our force every single moment in various strengths no matter it is action thought attitude feeling or temper, how can one match reflect at ease. Hence it hard to verify exactly what karmic coming from what deed.

To test the reaction, we can build up control source of some certain fate by following the lay of 5 Precepts which is general rules of deed limitation for a few years. Then intentionally break one of those rules to see them reflect which will be clearer now since we have controlled deed ready to compare head on.

The said 5 Precepts constitutes the basics of clean living which consists of abstinence from harming living beings, taking what is not given, sexual misconduct, lying and intoxication.

Even at this point, some may still be in an ignorant state on what all of this pressure is about, It's time to head straight to the point, we may conclude like this 'Any force energies or frequencies (you can refer back on sound of thought on Part 1) pushed out, will regularly return on similar source types, whatever good or bad action or behavior, happy or unhappy feeling, like or not like passion, love or hatred emotion. All these will come back right to the source, according to the rule of the natural movement of force, on no spatial surrounded hypothesis. Hence what one's did will reflect their fate that right to the way they live. If one love to fight, they'll get fight all the time, so most of their fate will be on the battlefield whether it is a real battlefield or business competition, we don't expect that such type of people will end up in the church taking chanting, meditation, cultivation or retreat unless life is too heavy.

Also, this assumption may apply to people who love horror movie will not be intoxicated by a love and romance film. Hence, their fate is destined by their own choice or preference, no one fixed or chose it for them.

If the nature of fate is like this, someone may question 'why numerous peoples went and died in the same event as Tsunami, Earthquake or War for example'. Did all of them initiate the same deed? The answer is 'no', passion or deed functionality convinced them or blinded them to those dead zones, the same scenario can be compared to an airport, no matter the purpose of their departure or destination, if one wants to go abroad they must go to the airport. Hence, the place, in this case, is just an interchange of destiny, one may be cut off by their own reflex and switch to the individual destination of life beyond, only one very being with precise perception on deed will know.

Anyway, after a very long matching, I have a few examples to share. Firstly, it was about a reflection or expression from a man or woman who had a love affair beyond their own spouse, disaster will fall upon their head. Their job, their finances, health, and family will collapse, it seems that all bad lucks were coming on them in unison wave after wave. I don't know exactly what kind of matching it is, maybe in term of frequency or calamity, but I can confirm this from my several years of curious observations. However, this kind of reflection will happen only on the good guy. For the one who is accustomed to casual love, is excluded from this logical assumption that their environment has developed into chaos like this from the beginning and don't feel that it is a problem. If one needs explanation, we may want to compare and conclude that casual love is simply immoral for some human beings while being natural for the others.

Another sample is a kind of good reflection in terms of finances which always happened to the Ono who graciously takes care of their parents. This is coming from several years of observation too.

The one who does not steal, exploit, encroach, and violate other people's right will not have the same reflection, so they can live in comfort, no need to take utmost caution on their assets or their love.

All these effects of deed can certainly be proved if you have 5

Precepts as your foundation all years round since this is precisely designed of 5 Precepts already limit all deeds that will bring back unwanted fate to us.

Be on this guide and we can be assured to live well.

Chapter 35

REINCARNATION

When a child is born, the body mass is always tiny. Once they grew up they became bigger and bigger from consumption of milk, meat, water, vegetable or mineral that is needed for body construction. That means the extra mass, in fact, doesn't belong to the child from the beginning. Indeed, it was transformed from pork, meat or fish. And if we claim that the only mass that is 'us' should be our originated body starting from the early stage in the mother's womb, it can be debated in the view of those fertilized cell that also came from the mother, since our first life is genuinely the only first nucleus which also came from mum and dad.

Such being the case, can we put it in this way that nothing belongs to us at all from the beginning. Before pig's mass is being transformed to ours, if one stabs the pig with a dagger, the pig will fight for survival, after being killed and becomes a pork, then the pork is being transformed to be part of our flesh, it alternatively, becomes our turn to reverse it. Does this mean that the 'Sense of Ownership' is an actual issue of fighting, not the mass themselves?

Thus, it is the problem of the subconscious that recognizes all mass as 'Self' which must be plotted...

Though nothing belongs to us, we still feel that we are somewhere in this body, but where?

Let's figure it out. If someone gets involved in a car accident and gets admitted, and got so unfortunate to have his limbs amputated, the doctor would have to replace his limbs with another, would he still be able to identify himself, the answer should be 'Yes'. Then, if the doctor takes off his heart and replace it with a new one, would he still be him, the answer still be 'Sure he is'. Thus one 'Self' is neither located on the limb nor heart. How About switching to a new head! if it is the case. The answer will be 'NO!', he is no longer himself. I think, we all concur!

The point is why do we all feel like that. it's due to the fact that we know exactly that our 'Self' is located in our head. Now let's focus on the head, if we remove our facial extras, like the eyes, ear, nose, hairs and even scalp, we all could feel the same that 'Self' is still there, not being removed accordingly. Thus, the only areas left is 'Brain' and we are rather confirmed by feeling that if the brain is being removed or replaced, there will be no 'US' in this body further, but where exactly in the brain, none can give an absolute answer yet, because most of us can vaguely feel that it is some kinds of illusory, intangible and ethereal somewhere in brain but not exactly the brain itself.

Could it be possible that our 'Self' is not simply a physical group of cells located somewhere in brain, but a tiny system that regulates on a certain brain network, whether it is Amygdala as 'Conscious Center' which responses are for survival, instincts, emotions or memory, which act like a Board of Director who always set requirement for profit and absorb all deeds regardless of profit or loss, then the Hypothalamus is as the center of 'Subconscious' who plays managing director's role, which interpreting from the requirement to the actual deal by linking between all nervous systems to the endocrine system via the Pituitary Gland, which will produces hormones that act as a messenger who carries command to various bodily-functions while having Hippocampus as a guide on how to function as the librarian who keep link index of all memories or database in all parts of brain that is necessary for matching in decision process.

Thus, the Question is where does this tiny system come from, if this is the case, the spiritual answer may be the way for this time around. We may refer this tiny system as an identical system or soul or spirit that came to install or do specific sequential arrangement right on DNA of the first fertilization cell with an absolute unique soul mark as the unique which has only one in the universe or the 'ONE', then any cell proliferation beyond this will carry this ID or identification all the way. Once there are any foreign ID cells invaded, our cells on those areas will instantly know since all cells conversed with each other all the time under team operation. Once alien cells are being spotted out, all nearby cells will alert all systems concerned for any necessary immune processes at once, and that's how our body knows when there are intruded cells that do not belong to us e.g. virus, bacteria, others people cells or organ whether it's the heart, kidney or limbs but not including red blood cells since they have no DNA and also anything in the digest system is not included, as those areas are restricted areas, nothing can intrude to the body system except 'the after digested ingredients' that is required for cell, energy and any other body operation materials production.

This is how sense of 'SELF' starts work with primal system, conscious and subconscious to manage all necessary functions for survival of the 'ONE', until the body expires, when there are no vital signals indicating LIFE for living further, thus the soul program leaves and implants on another appropriated cell, by generating specific frequency to a specific location of a newborn cell that do not yet has the soul mark implanted, correlated to auto mail wrapped up with our unique ID and necessary installation command that's being programmed to send out to appropriate recipient when a body dies or fails.

And this process is recognized as 'Reincarnation'. The system has only one goal that is 'Survival', and this is the only command that made it IMMORTAL.

For what 'Appropriated' means, we may use the concept of 'Frequency' to explain. Different frequency will fit on different receptor-like AM or FM for example. Frequency can go every-where regardless of distance. We can refer this to our mobile phone which can call exactly whatever location in the world if the right receptor is there.

One who left in peace may go to the more precise cell than a human being on peace area while one who left in pain or die in the fight may go to war zone instead. And if one who always spend their life on instinct, not on reason base, they may not have next chance on human cell, but to creatures that mostly use instinct, emotion or desire to carry on their natural life.

Unfortunately, memory doesn't go along with it, since the place to go has only one cell at the beginning, hence it's always startup with the only identical system on every sphere. That's why we can remember nothing of the past life. However, what's the meaning to have memories revolving since in fact there are less good memories than pain in almost every living thing that still struggling in 'SAMSARA' (wandering in the karmic cycle). And if we can have memories get along while our 'This Life' so suffering or even our past life may be something below human, do we still want to have memories revolved. Nature or Dhamma Always right on its rule.

On the conclusion, don't forget that before we came to this world, there is no 'US'. If it's true that there is no 'US' exist, then where do we came from.

Chapter 36

WHO FEARS DEATH

From last chapter of 'Reincarnation', we can see that life have their own system of maintaining eternity, but why do we still fear death, which is fact and unavoidable. We know exactly that life is a countdown from day one on earth, why do we still keep on fighting for this body till its last breath?

Genuinely, the one who has fear of death is not exactly the whole 'US'. It's just the conscious and the subconscious since these 2 intelligent substance stands only to mean 'SURVIVAL' of its body. Any factor that may lead to the end of its body will trigger an alarm to fight or run for its survival.

To have a clear picture, we may refer to the Subconscious as the Managing Director and Conscious as Board of Director while Self Identical System as an Investor.

The Board of Directors and Managing Director may fight to the death for company survival as both sticks to the company. But an investor is different, the investor may move to others once it's not worth to continue. Hence, the one who fears death is not totally the US since we consist of 3 systems. It depends on where we choose to be at which time if we attached to the consciousness or the subconscious on death threatening situations, we are the one who fears death, but if we choose to be on the identical system on the time, it's they who fear death not 'US'.

Last breath of life in fear, is only fluctuated by the frequency that can be generated, even the place to go may not be suitable for peace.

To choose the right site attached, once the time comes we need to practice and cultivate our release-gate to counter the subconscious auto gate.

Life with less threat is the happiest life. Let 's move to Part 3 of 'Life Editing' together for better living...

— PART 3 —

LIFE EDITING

From Part 1 and 2, we are already aware of how elusive the subconscious is involved in our involuntary pain, how it works, where it is located, the physical process done on our nerve cells on learning and our memory, how sensor and response gates is being cultivated, how auto response or reflection is being raised up through repeated actions of habituation or through shock of sensitization, how fate works, how life sometimes is being knocked down by unknown fate, or why we are at lost all the times by rage, grief, greed, love, fear or why we have to fight or run always, while others just sitting and playing joyfully, life is good on them without putting any efforts, and that's how reincarnation work.

Hence, we are no longer a naïve driver who only know just how to drive this body without any background knowledge.

We already realized on how destiny really lines up on the way we nurtured and fostered our subconscious which expressed out in term of behavior. If the fight is always the choice then fight fate was destined and vice versa if the flight is the top weight gate, then flight and fear life will be our fate.

Anyway, all this information will be just be another novels being invited to our brain with some exciting scenario, nothing in our life and destiny will be changed if we have no real perception, real faith, real action, real persistence, and endurance to edit what running out of track and liberate ourselves from the threat of the subconscious.

If someone asked me 'Did I achieve what I said in this book',

I can proudly say with an arrogance that 'No', however considering the much or little I have penned down, it's quite enough for me.

One should not wait to enjoy life until they reach multimillion wealth, happiness can start from multi-thousands if they know that they are on the right path of hope and certainly destined to millions at the end. Ten thousand miles always start from the first step. What we must do is 'Just Do It'. I love this Nike's phrase a lot, it encouraged me every time in seasons of discouragement, even on while I cultivate for or hesitate on whether I can truly edit my life and design my own destiny.

To Edit life and destiny, we need excellent mind frame to silently cultivate a new breed of subconscious precisely nurtured on a righteous path to share out nerve signal from the vicious gate of existing subconscious until it ceases to exist.

By the way, we are not life's programmer, we don't know the life programming syntax being coded and we have no efficacy to directly edit or code it on each individual cell. But what we do know is 'nature coded it by behavior', hence we can code or edit life program by well-designed behavior, the same way as nature did.

For example, to code or cultivate release-gates against the subconscious mental threat or body effect regardless of tensed - up nervous system, squeezing our heart, muscle contraction, fluctuation of blood flow, lack of oxygen, hard breathing, gastric contraction or any other responsive syndrome that try to push us do something to settle its grudge, we must have mindful perception on it, then release its action whenever it starts. But this may not be practical, since it is a fast track implanted gate on all nerve cells concerned, including a cell in spine and brain, like fiber optic which fastest in term of speed and volume of the signal transmitted (In term of physiology we may correlate this process to 'Negative Feedback'). What we can do on this stage is to signal this evil signal movement as fast as possible then release it on the way before it's functioning, thus pile up release gate to share out signal as much as possible from time to time until it can beat up those evil gates and release its signal on spot. However, we need to be faster and faster as we practice mindfully.

However, this was easier said than done. To achieve this we need time, we need persistence, we need a strong mind to endure all strike back of the subconscious since we leave this control task to them for a long time, once we want it back, it means WAR!

The Subconscious, by nature, has faith on what they did from the weight of longtime data collection like the one who got wealthy by deceit, it's hard to make him place his faith on a righteous path. Hence, all responsive gates lied in the same direction. And if we won't follow, for example, if it got rage and want revenge or got love and want to get love, but we consciously and consistently created another path to just silently release it, subconscious-initiated gates will find out that their function is not being committed well on responsive nerves, they will persistently send on signal and loop up more signal gates to tense up all actions in their direction which they already weighed as most potential solution, notwithstanding whatever fate or social effect we shall face or whatever mental or physical effect will be caused by such action, since its nature is linear programming. Thus, we must put all efforts to death, to endure all this seemingly endless strike back through the period until it ceased to persist, since the one who need to survive, or fear death is not us but the subconscious. If it continues to persist, it means harm to life, it will inhibit the process and flow to another solution path of its own survival functioning which we called this type of process as 'Positive Feedback'. However, if we lose by having some concerned, worry, fear or give up on the way, it means we added fuel on the fire. The Subconscious will become more confident and more vicious in its solution.

Such is the case, if we want to fight the wild ferocious subconscious with our mediocrity, we will certainly lose. Hence, we need to have a good frame of mind and tools.

Firstly , we need to weaken it by Fit and Give, then shield our fate with 5 Precepts, create a shelter for the spirit or righteous subconscious with Meditation, and weaponize it with Contemplation and Perception to transcend all illusions, lies and ignorance , then get Enlightenment or Awareness from all shades of evil subconscious, thus releasing and freeing ourselves from suffering and pain or even fear of death.

Chapter 37

FIT

Military dictatorship will have a greater role once the city is weak, in turmoil or in chaos, correlated to subconscious which will play a great role once we are on a weaker state.

Weakness doesn't mean just physical weakness, but also mental illness. Even a strong guy can easily be lost to depression, or strong will can easily be loosed to rage.

As it is in this case, the fitness of body and mind were basically needed if we want to weaken the power of the subconscious.

In this chapter, we shall attend on physical fitness first. For the later part we discuss mental fitness, subsequently, we shall also talk on 'Meditation'.

Compare the body to a car, if we just parked it forever what will happen. Firstly, the battery shuts down, tires become flatten and inflexible, lubricant losses due to leaks, all mechanics become stiffened, exhaust system experiences deterioration etc. Hence if we put our body on the same state, similar situation will also happen, since our body or muscle is also fiber, no different from tires, the more we use our muscles, the more blood flows, then more oxygen is carried through our blood on supporting cells burn for energy generation, hence, heat will be generated, old cell flexible like body massage, and stimulate new flexible cell proliferate to replace the burning one. Those areas which are not much utilized, there will be no cell replacement and the old cells will become more stiffened and will be withering and decaying as the day goes by.

It's true that cell burn made life short since cell proliferation was not limited, but DNA to templated cell proliferation was limited. Anyway, to stay under standby mode like Ford case in Part 1, I don't think we love it. Thus, the good concept is to utilize our body to its utmost effect with happiness through to the end no matter the duration. Quality is, however, better than quantity, especially for life and living.

By the way fitness training associated with cell burn does not certainly lead to a shorter lifespan compared to idleness and laxity, because no matter the situation, man cannot stay idle, they need to do something, even if it's not fitness training, exercise or sport, they would still think, may be much more than normal people, and if such is the case, their brain cells may go first, since it's been used maximally, and probably 20 hrs per day. while physical exercise may take at most 2-3 hrs. daily. In that case, the one who sits and is idle has the chance to go first resulting from brain deterioration and that ultimately leads to body failure, despite a very long lifespan remain on other cells section.

To make the body fit, there are many ways that we all know, whether it is running, swimming, biking etc. For 1-2 hrs. a day, life will surely be out of its weakened state, no allergy no depression, regular blood flow, all parts flexible with cells refreshed. I hope no one will argue against these points since everybody knows how useful it is for daily exercise, but there is no motivation since nobody knows how it affects our destiny.

For exercise, my favorite is jogging. Beside it can fit up our body, we also gain experience in fighting with the subconscious. Whether you are an experienced runner or a mediocre, starting from 1-5 Km, battle with the subconscious is unavoidable since its duty is trying every effort to save energy, save cells for a longer span, but we going to waste it. The Subconscious will instigate us to stop, to give up, it's so tired, it can no longer go on, heart about to collapse, muscles burning to death, we're going to die, stop for water please and so on.

The Subconscious will persist like this for a while until we endure and overwhelms it, depending on each individual strength based on our physical and mental state, then it will retreat from time to time to the last frontier which supposed to be a real threat to the body for actual damage.

80-90% of the subconscious threat is illusionary, if we can endure till we are able to release it naturally for all, we can also relax on 80-90% illusive troubles too.

The way to fight subconscious is not far from what one must fight if they want to be free from drug addiction.

Chapter 38

GIVE

Before starting the big war, weakening our enemy as much as possible is the best concept. 'Giving' is also one technique for weakening the subconscious will, since its nature is to keep everything for life support.

The more we take, the more we possess, the more we guard our life support, and the more a fighting fate can be expected.

Hence, giving induces loss of appetite for possessions and guarding, which is the best strategy.

And by this giving path, our will upgrade from mediocrity to veteran in fighting with the subconscious, then gains good fate for our destiny which is the resultant effect, since what we get will be what we give or what goes around, comes around.

On giving, we made someone happy and we are also happy to see them happy. Once we get back something unexpected because of our giving we are also happy. Hence, we get triple prizes with half effort.

But On the contrary, if we took from someone by force and we lose something by chance, we faced lose on both ends, with some enemies added up to the piles.

If above is the case, then it's worthy for one to cultivate giving as a lifestyle thus preventing the subconscious from running into a perpetual selfishness.

By the way, giving also have modes of practice. One cannot just give all out from the beginning, it sounds too crazy and the subconscious will fight to the death even if we directly challenge it like that.

To fight with the subconscious over possession we need to lure them first with something that sounds reasonable, like start giving out the over a year used or unused possessions, since we can give the reason for the unused properties that over the year it has not been utilized. it's not wise, it occupies our limited area and lessens our comfort. Hence, improve your comfort and space by giving it out to someone who may need it and receive a double favor. Like this subconscious will weigh between 2 gains and 1 minor loss pathways, then the signal will flood more to the main gates and no loop will persist on a fight

If we keep on doing like this from time to time, our giving gate will be cultivated continuously and becomes a normal behavior or our nature finally.

Once you become a giver, our charm will rise, and the chance of opportunity will come on their own without much struggling, and that will be our new fate.

On giving, the choice is ours, We can give whatever we want to whoever we wish and whenever we are happy. But the receiver or taker has no choice, they must fight for it or wait for luck which normally does not come free to the one who never gives.

Chapter 39

FIVE PRECEPTS

After weakening the subconscious with certain training and a giving attitude, now it's time to fight. But we cannot just go and fight in an unorthodox manner, we need weapons and shield.

Fitness training and Giving is just an internal strategy to weaken the subconscious with good fate as the effect of a giving attitude.   However, both of this tool is never a guarantee that our life will not be knocked down by unknown fate since our fate depends on our deeds or behavior which most ignorantly originated from the subconscious autopilot. We, therefore, need to shield our fate with behavioral control. Such as the case, we need some reliable guide of behavior to guarantee that by doing this or not doing that, will not bring back bad luck or unwanted fate to us.

For me, 5 Precepts is the guide that I do follow as usual. It is the general rules of deed limitation that is precisely designed to cover and shield against all deeds that will bring back unhappiness to us. This constitute the basics of clean living which is abstainance from:

1. Harming living beings

2. Stealing or take whatever that's not being given

3. Sexual misconduct

4. Lying

5. Intoxication

By just not commit only this 5, it means great war declared since we all know the difficulty by avoiding all these precepts.

The Subconscious survival functionality always chooses to harm others rather harm themselves if it's coming to that choice.

Taking advantage of others to support your own comfort is also a basic idea of our society.

Having sex is the profound base of survival, since life needs a reproduction of physical body to support soul implant on reincarnation process, regardless of whoever they are or has as its possessor or not. Especially son or daughter of heaven is the most tamper or passionate since quality is a profound requirement for body production.

The lie is also unavoidable when the truth means a disadvantage in any way.

Intoxication/drunkenness is always needed, for social purposes, for relaxation from tension, to release us from a problem for a while, or even dull our brain to ignore the truth which barely accepts us for who are we, what we are living for, where do we go after this.

We all know that all these 5 deeds are not the righteous path, and we know that we shouldn't do that to others. None loved is to be harmed, to be cheated, to have a loved one being abused, to lie or to be in a dull state. However, for the sake of self-survival we often helplessly do it nevertheless to one or all, even if it's against our will especially for the righteous one. Hence, it's war!

Once we have committed ourselves to follow these 5 precepts, the war between the consciousness and our subconscious will happen anywhere anytime.

Inhibit gate or control gate will be configured for all over synapses from time to time. The more we can win on inhibiting subconscious signal flow, the more we are on righteous track and the more we are on good fate with less enmity. And since we are quasi-good guy, more chance and opportunity will come to us on trust base.

Who will not prefer to deal with the one they can trust that will not harm, steal, take advantage or lie to them?

Also, the one clear from intoxication will have a clear mind that can think and see everything more precise, hence can find more opportunities.

After a while, once proof revealed itself by real feedback of good fate from good deed accordingly, the subconscious evil gate will die out consecutively since righteous gate raised up rate is higher than the repeated evil gate, then we become veteran on LIFE EDITING, and ready to encounter the great war of meditation.

If we not lost in the faith of fight in this war, with our absolute endurance and persistence over the years, we will find out ourselves that fate really can be edited. Life will become more peaceful and comforting by itself, no much struggling needed.

This doesn't mean money or wealth but its real happiness like heaven is now on our side.

Chapter 40

MEDITATION

Though Fitness training and Giving can weaken the subconscious power while 5 Precepts can fight subconscious and shield our fate to some extents, it's still not enough to line up against all emotions or auto response of the evil subconscious.

To have a firm fight, we need a home or shelter. If one is so tired from work they will think of home to rest, one who flees on fear will directly run to the home as it feels safe there. As against the strong wind, icy or scorching sun, we run home for warmth, on a very lonely state we are back home to family. And all of these is the reason for having a home. Most of us have a physical home for our body but very few have homes for the spirit. Hence, we need to cultivate it up so we can ignore all evil persistence, sigh after furious fight, retreat from rage, refuge from depression, stay in peace and calm, rest, relax, recover, recuperate and give us moment for conscious to contemplate and strike back on best righteous path that will bring back no harm to us.

One who has a home or shelter is, however, better than a homeless guy. Homeless one can fight nothing no matter how wealthy he is, how strong he was or so great to the sky, correlating to the Giant Titanic in the sea which is incomparable to a small boat on a shore!

To have a shelter, we need to build it up through Meditation.

Once we talk about Mediation most people will think of sitting with closed eyes, releasing all stresses, then breathing with focus and create a mindfulness. During that time, fighting between focus and distractions will engage in a fierce battle. More practice, ensures more success, more peace, more calm, more mindfulness and more happiness. However, we cannot manage to have this traditional warfare all the time since the subconscious's tactic is guerrilla warfare with ambushes, sabotage, raids, petty warfare, hit-and-run tactics. Once emotion instantly emerges, how can we just instantly sit and close our eyes? Thus, meditation is what we must practice all the time whether we are sitting walking or working. We must infiltrate, invade or penetrate the subconscious operation all the ways so that we can gain space by sharing from them.

Some may refer that how can one meditate all the time, we must work, we have to think, there are numerous things we need to do. The fact is that we normally lose our mind to all the things all the times, the chance for recalling is very minute even when we try all out to keep it on track all the way, thus we have no need to worry about that, the subconscious is famous on capturing the flag. However, by a strong intention to maintain mediation like this, we are at least have all the time 'control' to check out once the subconscious sneakily attacked us on its illusive purposes for we can release or relax it on time since it is an unwanted action that we want to render void, it is to avoid further repetition of suffering and pain that made the subconscious stronger.

By the way, if one can really maintain their senses or mindfulness all the time, then one has no further need to be concerned over everything since enlightenment will lead their life through perfect destiny by itself.

Now let's see Meditation on a deeper dimension, as to how to proceed and how it works. Besides Breathing and Focusing, Meditation has plenty of methods regardless of the Focus on some certain substances like colors, water or fire, to gain emotions, on the character of each substance ; Corpse Contemplation to have concept of body after death that it is that's all for life; Recollection on Sacred substance to perceive their tranquility and goodness; Mindfulness on death, breathing or impurity of the body to perceive it; Entering the Sublime States of Mind to purify our heart; and many more. However, the most basic one that can instantly put in action efficiently is sense or feeling on breathing since it is a very profound tool existing for us to pick up at all time and it is very sensitive and fluctuates that really fit for mindfulness practice to gains concept of breathing which reflects emotion or subconscious work on each single moment.

In fact the way to be mindful of breathing is not 'Focus' but

'Sense', 'Feel' or 'Know' it causes 'Focus' on normal people, will use their eyes to eye on breathing in - breathing out, even on closed eyes, that possibly lead to tense on the acupoint between brows if meditation persist for period of time, since all muscles around eyes ball will move up and down all the times until it tense to contraction and pain. So just feel it once it breathes in and feels it once it breathes out.

At first, it may be difficult to just 'Feel' since it's always losses to 'Focus' or 'Daydream' on every moment only within the first few breaths. But we must persist and endure to just feel it whenever we have a chance, whether we are sitting, walking, sleeping or when available from all works or thoughts. The purpose is to cultivate our home for the spirit. After days, months, years passed through cultivation like this whether we win or lose on the way, we at least gain the breathing memory day by day until someday we shall no further be a homeless spirit but will finally have 'Home' to rest, recuperate, retreat or refuge.

If 'Feel' is mindfulness or conscious and 'Focus' is autonomic or subconscious, feel breathing will be where engagement between the conscious and subconscious started. Our mission is to capture the flag and gain more gate on the nerve to cultivate another breathing path or memory to become righteous subconscious that will certainly bring no harm back to us no matter at present or future. And this breathing memory will be our 'Home' or 'Shelter'.

To amplify what kind of fighting is going on during engagement, let's see sample of repeated counting of 1, 2, 3, 4 in our mind continuously for a while, the subconscious will sneakily replace itself on counting, even while we already stop counting, still we can hear its count on its own for a while. The Subconscious is the best assistant but unfortunately, it has no righteous sense, thus many things assisted by them are out of the track, whether it's social, goodness, righteous or fear. Our duty is to sense if it is our count or its count, if we can feel that it is its count, not ours that means we have already transcended its sneaking then we gain one gate of release or awakening which will become a brick for our spiritual home. Hence home for spirit is not exactly breathing path or memory, in fact, it is 'Release or Awakening Memory'. As for breathing sense, we gain nothing from it, but what we gain is awakening or release spot once be able to recall back from 'Focus' or 'Daydream' which being sneakily stolen the thunder from our 'Feel' or 'Sense'. The more we can capture the sneak, the bigger shelter being cultivated which mean we have more gate on nerve cells to leak subconscious strong signal flow which will lead to release of all emotions by sharing signal out through our 'Release Gate' instead and this will sooner or later become 'Positive Feedback' or 'Solution of Everything' noted down on new blood subconscious which will auto operate once there are unwanted tenses caused by vicious subconscious, like 'Set a thief to catch a thief'.

Besides, this cultivated shelter can be our 'Release Gate' from the evil subconscious, if we can practice to the level, it also can be 'Relax Gate' or big shelter where we can take refuse or ignore the subconscious force, thus leaving our mind free on resting state, eventually entering standby mode. Under standby mode, we shall be on a very happy state of absolute release, no pain, no trouble, and no illusion caused. The subconscious has no influence under this mode as it already lost major signal through this path.

To trigger our mind to this standby mode, we just go back to our initial feeling for realizing that which we always practice on, thus the release signal will flood through the spinal cord to the brain and the brain will signal all functions to enter temporary hibernation mode that preserves all energy usages to minimum and then we are at rest.

To prove that we can reach this stage of being able to designate our mind to this temporary hibernation mode, just to see it physically, if we have goosebumps after entering this release mode then it is. Under real standby mode, all temperature and energy will be preserved to a minimum by pulling down body hairs to save heat or energy, not let it out, like goosebumps once we are cold.

Meditation is not limited to breathe sensitivity, if one is not comfortable on how he breaths, they may place their mind on each individual sacred that they have faith with and practice to know once image loss then recalls back or doing both at the same time by place their mind on their own sacred image and feel breathing altogether. Once the sacred image is lost and remains only breathing that means we are being stealth the thunder already, the subconscious sneakily captures the flag, we then recall back to the origin status where we have our sacred image and feel breathing. So, the image is in a stable control while fighting on , breath feeling is fluctuating, like swimming with life tube through a strong wind, if we keep focussing on the tube while contemplating the wave, we will rather be assured that we shall not be easily lost in the wave.

Absolute image concentration is good for a novice, the image is still a substance, no movement, and fluctuations, we can contemplate only on loss and appear while breathing is different. it moves and fluctuates with effect from the subconscious operation or emotion, with fighting with it, we can gain more experience, skills, perception, and concept, correlating it to punching the sandbag, however, it's greatness cannot be compared to a real fight. The trick is what we need to recognize who we must fight with all the time and not loss conscious to it.

To create a great shelter or spirit home we need to meditate like this on any available period once it loses to daydream try to recall back. At first, we may be able to recall only 2-3 times a day, after a period of practice it may become 10-20 until 100-200 and that's great.

Keep up the practice like this until this shelter is solid and be where we can easily really rely on to instantly retreat from fear, grieve, greed, rage depress or even lovesick once it attacks.

If we can retreat like this till it becomes our instinct, then it will auto trigger once we are going to leave this body we shall not fear much, thus launch from this shelter in peace. Though up to this stage of meditation we may not reach the enlightenment to understand the truth of life, our appropriated destiny will not be so bad since our last move signal is well defined, the place to go will not be rough since tranquil delicate frequency or spirit unmatched to turmoil place, and on the contrary turmoil frequency also not possible to get lucky draw moving to well precise place too.

Through practice, the more we can overwhelm the subconscious through this intended cultivation, the more we gain control back from its negative feedback. There is no harm at all to cultivate righteous subconscious through meditation. Some may refer that if we just always keep running away from the problem to shelter, how can we overcome it. This is not really true, if we are on dull state or fuzzy with problem how can we get any good idea, but if we are just relaxed from stress for a brief moment, we can eventually have time to search the best way out and can solve problem more effectively, it's is compared to one who forgets the name of a well-known famous superstar and persist to think it out all the times until few hours passed with no outcome, thus rest their mind to 'Just forget it', and only brief moment after that they got to know it instantly like a popup result. It is like this because, on thinking, they give no chance for the brain to search, we have one brain and the brain has schedules like the CPU schedules, if we keep on the consistent click, then it stunned or hang and led to final crazy trump card of 'Ctrl + Alt + Del' thus shut it all, no good outcome gets. Instead, if we stop to persistently click and give the CPU a time for the search to get queue on schedule, then the result can be picked up.

Most people know that once we are in a storm of emotion, we need to keep cool, keep calm so that we can find the way out, but very few persons can do that, it's easier said than done because they want to instantly be the champion who can knock a vicious enemy with their mediocrity .

Chapter 41

CONTEMPLATION AND PERCEPTION

Cultivation of 'Release- Gate' or 'Home for Spirit' is only Part 1 of meditation, there's still Part 2 of advance meditation that is Contemplation and Perception, the Law and Concept, then transcend the truth. Since all problems caused by 'Ignorance' of how the subconscious works, to exactly overcome the problem is 'Transcendent', not only just release it and it's fine since that will be an endless war.

Compare the subconscious to the spoilt kid, once they behaved out of the track, then we put them in jail, once they are out, their will, still no change since they don't know exactly what's wrong or why they are put in jail.

It's true that we can limit their bad action for a while, but we cannot edit their attitude if we do not let them get to know what led to this negative feedback that brings back all bad to them instead of comfort as they thought. Once the kid transcends its ignorance then their choice will be a righteous one and there will be no further evil deed being initiated, and that is called

'Enlightenment'.

Enlightenment is a logic that will pop up by itself, no one can enlighten by force, by learning or understanding, because enlightenment is the consequence or product of transcendence by one knowing the truth until it overwhelms all ignorance.

We need to know what the truth is or what is elusive first. Not all we feel is the truth as we already learned a lot from Part 1 of the Subconscious. So before enlightening, we need to disintegrate the subconscious by just contemplating its action, emotions or will that concern all involuntary actions, and get perception and comprehend the law and concept of why they do that or this, is it reasonable, is it righteous.? And ponder on all the ways through its effects, then distinguish it out on what brought back happiness or what carried back illness. Joy also can be classified as an illness since its excitement led to a new wave of passion, not peace and calm, or relax state like happiness.

After contemplating like this for a certain period, many ill intents will be caught up and weakened or inhibited from our transcendence that led to positive feedback being implanted and cultivated from time to time until its evil gate is being overwhelmed by new righteous one, and no longer have much gate remaining to persist since cell dies every day, if no repetition for a while such system of the signal path will fade away. And if we continue to cultivate our perception like this for a long time we shall comprehend the concept of survival and be able to guide our subconscious to the correct path. Until then our habit that keep on always observing every activity of the subconscious as trace and track will become our profound personality. And by this habit of observation, we will become 'Observer' someday and no further an 'Actor'. See outside the box get more novel perspective. We will always clear on others behavior but very indistinctive on our own cause we are always an actor. Since vision changed, we shall see whatever we never see, we shall know why people are doing this or that, we shall know their deed and fate since what they do is product of their subconscious which no different from us because we are all human race with the same gene or same living function that needs to fight for survival on the same methodology. People are being distinguished by face, by character, by personality, and by behavior, not because we have the different gene or different on a profound base. Indeed, we all have the same gene or set of profound functions on our DNA, but the difference is on each individual functioning location that makes us unique, and different on social and environmental base which also makes us unique on behavioral tendency while we all are basically required to do the same for survival, but some righteous will do differently the from vicious ones. So, if we know ourselves from raw thinking, then we also understand others too.

When the time of full comprehension of the above concept comes, it means we are already on a starting point of enlightenment. I really feel or admit that the subconscious is not us nor others true self but it's the one who played with our lives all the time. 80% of illness whether it's mental or physical including fear of death is initiated by them with no consent from us.

If we have passed up to this point, what remain for the rest is just to continue on Fitness, Giving, and taking 5 Precepts, Meditation and Contemplations all the times, to maintain good health, good life and happiness all the way till final enlightenment is saturated and pops up to know that it's just a system that's understandable for either us or others, and know what goes around comes around for every deed, hence, we are fully aware of the concept of 'IT IS WHAT IT IS' and transcends the truth of THINGS, no more illusions to be faced with.

Chapter 42

GUARDIAN ANGEL

Now, let's see why someone have to be with them or have their own Guardian Angel. From Kate's case of millipede, her vicious subconscious, built-up Demon from millipede, it does not make sense to others but it's true for her! Hence, the truth is belonging to one with such perception. If some other person since birth has never seen an electric fan non-operational and someone tries to convince them that in fact the fan just has 3-4 blades not a round plate as they usually saw it while rotating , how can they believe it, and if winding is as fast as the speed of light, what will be their perception. Hence, no one can really confirm the exact truth from what they see. Such is the case when a demon is created by the vicious subconscious, A Guardian Angel is created under a righteous subconscious by our 5 tools of fitness, giving, 5 precepts, meditation, and contemplation, which must be real too!

Viciousness can do many evils that we don't know as we already learnt a lot from Part 1, the righteous also can do the same but on an opposite level, whether we are guided unto the correct path or a warning if we are out of track, even we can receive some premonitions of what will happen before we or our beloved one misconduct something. Nothing can instantly emerge without initial frequency. The sound of Righteous is always an option to follow.

However, such warning from the righteous is quite thin and will pop up only on some precious occasion, while a vicious subconscious is out of duty like on a very short moment of wake up while the conscious is still not fully operational or on the meditative-release moment. However, this thin signal will be amplified through our long cultivation. Until then, we shall really have our true Guardian Angel who will take care of us through our long journey.

Most people know once life struck we need, consciousness; mindfulness; awareness; awakening or enlightening, as the best way to keep life smooth, but less people know how to make it true, how to edit our life path, how to handle other's subconscious or how to settle deadlock quiz of why we are here, what we are living for, where will we go and do after our existence here on earth.

And this is all about 'LIFE EDITING'.

Enlightenment will settle for us once we aware that all these troubles are for the subconscious, not us, hence, we have nothing to deal with it and that's all.

It is truly an honor that you read my work. I Hope all these knowledge will be helpful to you. I dare not confirm that everything I wrote in this book is 100% correct because the samples and corresponding control used by me is to identify the solution and relative responses, which are exclusive to me and my family, including some close friend that I thought I knew their lives well.

It's just trying to share my knowledge and experience, perhaps it can be of help for someone like me, who tried to figure out who played with our lives and what is the best way to live well.

For me and my family, the result is quite impressive. Our family group's name on the social network is 'Happy Family'.

Respectfully,
Veerachai Junhunkit
saengdham@gmail.com